[handwritten notes:]
p9 ISA registration
p28 risk assessment
p29 insurance
p30 hire agreement
p63 food workers
p68 staffing levels
p70 cond

Protecting All God's Children

The Policy for Safeguarding Children
in the Church of England

4th edition 2010

CHURCH HOUSE
PUBLISHING

© *The Archbishops' Council 2010*

Fourth impression 2010

Published in 2010 for the House of Bishops of
the General Synod of the Church of England

Church House Publishing
Church House, Great Smith Street,
London, SW1P 3AZ.

ISBN 978 0 7151 1051 5

Printed and bound in Great Britain
by Halstan & Co, Amersham

For a downloadable electronic version of the
full document for local, non-commercial use,
please consult the Church of England website.

British Library Cataloguing in Publication data

A catalogue record for this book is available
from the British Library

Contents

Foreword

by the Archbishops of Canterbury and York

We are delighted to commend this fully revised and updated House of Bishops' policy on safeguarding children. The Church of England has had a child protection policy since 1995 and this document builds on previous good work. We are pleased to note that dioceses, parishes and church officers at all levels continue to grow in commitment and confidence, seeking to continually update their good practice and to respond well to concerns when they arise.

Our children deserve the best care that the Church can provide. We rejoice in the time and devotion given by so many people, ordained and lay, paid and volunteers, to the exciting challenge of nurturing our children and young people within the Church.

Since the last edition of *Protecting All God's Children* was published in 2004, we have developed our understanding of both the importance of safeguarding adults who may be vulnerable, and careful selection of those who work with children and vulnerable adults. The Church of England published *Promoting a Safe Church*, our policy for safeguarding adults, in 2006. The House of Bishops has just approved as well the third important policy on vetting and safer recruitment, which will be published as an interim policy pending resolution of the new Government's review into these matters. These three policies reflect our growing theological and pastoral endeavour, underpinning the value of safeguarding as part of the life and ministry of the church. Together, the policies provide the basis for ensuring that we provide the safest possible environment for everyone to grow and to flourish. Nothing less will do in a community called to witness to the eternal dignity of every human being, and which seeks to embrace Jesus' teaching about the importance of children in his kingdom.

Since 2004, the Government has twice revised its foundation document *Working Together to Safeguard Children*. The most recent version (2010) affirms that churches 'have an important role in safeguarding children and supporting families'. Churches are expected to have procedures for responding properly to safeguarding concerns, appropriate codes of practice for those working directly with children, and procedures that are in accordance with safer recruitment guidance. This version of *Protecting All God's Children* is our response to this challenge.

We thank God for all our children, and for those who nurture them in the faith, and pray that we may faithfully and joyfully fulfil our responsibilities towards them.

✠ Rowan Cantuar:

✠ Sentamu Ebor:

Principles of the House of Bishops' Policy for Safeguarding Children

Every person has a value and dignity which comes directly from the creation of male and female in God's own image and likeness. Christians see this potential as fulfilled by God's re-creation of us in Christ. Among other things this implies a duty to value all people as bearing the image of God and therefore to protect them from harm.

Principles

We are committed to:

- The care, nurture of, and respectful pastoral ministry with, all children and all adults

- The safeguarding and protection of all children, young people and adults when they are vulnerable

- The establishing of safe, caring communities which provide a loving environment where there is a culture of 'informed vigilance' as to the dangers of abuse.

We will carefully select and train all those with any responsibility within the Church, in line with safer recruitment principles, including the use of criminal records disclosures and registration with the relevant vetting and barring schemes.

We will respond without delay to every complaint made which suggests that an adult, child or young person may have been harmed, co-operating with the police and local authority in any investigation.

We will seek to work with anyone who has suffered abuse, developing with him or her an appropriate ministry of informed pastoral care.

We will seek to challenge any abuse of power, especially by anyone in a position of trust.

We will seek to offer pastoral care and support, including supervision and referral to the proper authorities, to any member of our church community known to have offended against a child, young person or vulnerable adult.

In all these principles we will follow legislation, guidance and recognized good practice.

1. Introduction

Aims and purpose

1.1　The purpose of this policy document is to identify and outline the issues and principles of safeguarding children for the Church of England.

- At a national level[1] it is the House of Bishops which approves the policy and provides recommended procedures where it is judged that the Church of England should have common practice across the dioceses.

- Building on this, dioceses may provide additional procedures and examples of good practice to give further substance to the House of Bishops' policy so that those authorized volunteers, employed laity and people holding the Bishop's licence, can properly and with confidence engage with children.

1.2　A companion policy document[2] deals with the issues of safeguarding vulnerable adults.

1.3　Note that the term 'child' is used throughout this document for the sake of simplicity to cover both children and young people under the age of eighteen. In direct work it will usually be more appropriate to use the term 'young people' for those over the age of eleven.

1.4　The Church is not an arm of the state but works with statutory agencies to help safeguard children. There are therefore many references to statutory provisions in this policy. But the Church also reserves the right to take its own view of statutory schemes, and, while always remaining within the law, to argue for changes or to express disagreement.

1.5　Since its first child protection policy, and before, the Church has taken the view that matters which are the subject of statutory provisions should be brought to the relevant agencies for determination. This is particularly important if there is a possible need for statutory action to protect a child or adult, or to bring an alleged offender to justice

Our theological approach

1.6　Every human being has a value and dignity which comes directly from the creation of male and female in God's own image and likeness. Christians see this potential fulfilled by God's re-creation of us in Christ. Among other things this implies a duty to value all people as bearing the image of God and therefore to protect them from harm. Christ saw

---

[1] 'national level' should be read to include those parts of the Church of England outside England with different legislation, e.g. the Diocese of Sodor and Man, the Diocese in Europe, and the Channel Islands which was attached to the Diocese of Winchester. They should implement this policy as far as they are able but may need to adapt parts of it.

[2] *Promoting a Safe Church*, House of Bishops, 2006.

children as demonstrating a full relationship with God. He gave them status, time and respect.

1.7 Every person is equally precious to God. Each one needs the assurance that respect for this brings. Individuals who suffer abuse often experience a loss to their identity and worth; there is often shame and a misplaced guilt. The Church is intended to be a place where men, women and children, including those who are hurt and damaged, may find healing and wholeness. It is our calling to be agents of healing and recovery in such a way that enables all who have suffered from abuse to lead lives with dignity in a context that is as safe as possible. It is about speaking words of peace. It is communication of 'shalom'; that is, of justice, healing and peace for the whole of the individual, as well as for the community.

1.8 God is present and at work in the world in many ways. A Church empowered by the Holy Spirit is especially a place where the wonderful character of God is manifested. The Church is called to witness to that truth. As individual Christians and as part of the Church, our vocation is to reflect the character of God. We are called to welcome and care for the oppressed, the marginalized, and the victims of injustice. Safeguarding good practice concerns the development of safer expressions of care to all and underpins the love and welcome of God for all people.

1.9 Justice is part of the outworking of love. The Church must hold in tension concerns for both justice and compassion. Nevertheless, those who have suffered child abuse have sometimes found an unsympathetic hearing. They may be disbelieved, discouraged and damaged further. Some people may side with the alleged perpetrator. This occurs in all parts of society, but it is particularly hurtful when it occurs within the Church. Such actions compound the sense of injustice that many feel. In answer to the question 'What does God require of us?' the need to act justly is set alongside the need to love mercy and to walk humbly with God (Micah 6.8).

1.10 Many who have endured child abuse consider that mercy towards those who have sinned is set above the need for the victims to be enabled to find justice. Both are essential. In creating humankind God made us to be together, to live in community. When one suffers we all suffer. We are all made poorer by every incidence of child or adult abuse as by all sin. In finding the grace to act righteously towards those who suffer, we also experience transformation through grace. We become better people and our churches become safer places for all.

1.11 In similar ways, offenders may also be assured that they are precious to God, and find healing and wholeness. Because redemption and the possibility of forgiveness are so central to the gospel, the Church is not only well equipped to assist in the rehabilitation of offenders but is also challenged by the issues their presence raises for us. The Church is part of a society where collusion with violence in families, emotional abuse or certain taboos on sexual abuse often holds sway. It is our calling to hold on to both justice and grace and to build safer church communities, often in challenging circumstances. Church people have sometimes required those who have suffered abuse to forgive. We need to understand forgiving and receiving forgiveness as lifelong processes.

1.12 Our congregations can be a refuge for those who have perpetrated abuse but are seeking help in maintaining a non-abusive way of life. We have also to be aware that some who abuse may see church membership as an opportunity to be close to children or vulnerable parents in order to continue their abusive patterns of behaviour. Experience shows that whether penitent or not, those who abuse need support in taking responsibility for their own actions and in stopping their abusive behaviour: in addition, of course, the vulnerable need protection from them. The genuine penitent will accept the need for careful arrangements, including some restrictions, for his or her return to church fellowship. This is in line with the Church's realistic understanding of sin and its effects, and the Church's responsibility to love all God's people.

1.13 The Gospel accounts remind us of Jesus' humanity and vulnerability throughout his life. He gave up all but the power of love. He gave up wealth, security and status. He listened to and ministered to those who were powerless and vulnerable; he appointed fallible and weak disciples who needed to discover their limitations and find strength by living in God's grace with each other. Those who are humble and vulnerable themselves are often gifted with a ministry with those who are most in need, including with children and adults who have suffered. There is therefore a challenge for the Church to encourage ministry, service and leadership in ways that promote discernment of one's boundaries and limitations, reliance on God and our brothers and sisters in Christ, thus developing compassionate, collaborative and enabling ministries which value careful listening to all.

1.14 Child abuse is a scourge on individuals, on our Church and in our society and we must name it as such, doing everything we can to prevent it. We are to nurture children as fully as we can in Christ's name.

1.15 A Christian approach to safeguarding children will therefore expect both individuals and communities to:

- create a safe environment for children and their families;
- act promptly on any complaints made;
- care for those who have been abused in the past;
- minister appropriately to those who have abused;
- provide opportunities for healing and flourishing.

1.16 God's mission is a message of good news to love and welcome the poor and marginalized. The Church must take seriously both human propensities to evil but also the God-given resources of goodness, peace, healing and justice: in short, God's love, God's life.

Societal context

1.17 The abuse of children is often dominated by sensational and misleading press and media coverage. Safeguarding is about the welfare and the protection of children. This is something the whole Church should be concerned about and engaged in through developing and supporting good practice and responding appropriately when harm occurs. The Government, local authorities, schools and the wider statutory sector have in recent years sought to promote safeguarding within a holistic, multi-agency approach to children and families, for example through the *Every Child Matters* programme and the Children Act 2004. The Government's foundation policy document, *Working Together to Safeguard Children*, which addresses interagency and multi-agency working for the welfare and protection of children, has been revised twice since 2004 when the previous edition of *Protecting All God's Children* was issued.

1.18 The Bichard Inquiry report and work on the Safeguarding Vulnerable Groups Act 2006 has applied safer recruitment principles across both the voluntary and statutory sectors. Among a good deal of additional guidance, particular mention should be made of *Safeguarding Children and Safer Recruitment in Education* 2007 and the Children's Workforce Development Council guidance *Recruiting Safely* 2009 for the voluntary sector.

1.19 In addition, Local Safeguarding Children's Boards (LSCBs) have been established to ensure that faith groups, among others, respond adequately to the demands of safeguarding, and Local Authority Designated Officers (LADOs) have been appointed; their duties include advising faith groups on the management of children's workers who are alleged to have harmed children. A Children's Commissioner has also been appointed.

1.20 Recent years have therefore seen many changes, with an extension of statutory requirements and tightened procedures across the children's workforce in all sectors.

1.21 There can be an unhelpful emphasis on sexual abuse in society when physical abuse, emotional abuse and neglect, sometimes alongside domestic violence, are more common. All abuse is more likely to occur in families or to be perpetrated by extended family relatives or friends. This presents a challenge to the church and to society, to engage with safeguarding children as a whole.

Ecumenical context

1.22 In the Churches there is a continuing growth in ecumenical agreement and co-operation on safeguarding, especially between the Methodist Church and the Church of England, as part of the outworking of the Covenant. Our continued participation in Churches' Agency for Safeguarding and the Christian Forum for Safeguarding is of great benefit in building and maintaining relations with all Churches, especially the Baptist Union of Great Britain and the United Reformed Church; the Society of Friends; the Catholic Church of England and Wales (and particularly CSAS[3]); the Salvation Army; the Church of Scotland; the Assemblies of God and the independent charity Churches Child Protection Advisory Service. Furthermore, these bodies enable and enhance our participation in discussions with government departments and agencies.

---

[3] The Catholic Safeguarding Advisory Service.

1.23   We have learned from each other and especially from those who have had
        thorough scrutiny of practice and procedures. The following key values
        or approaches[4] are regarded as important underpinning for our
        safeguarding practice:

- the child's welfare is paramount;

- prevention is vital;

- transparency;

- accountability;

- partnership with statutory authorities;

- use of independent specialist advice;

- the active management of risk;

- a 'One Church' approach;

- a culture of informed vigilance.

Descriptions and definitions

1.24   A **child** is defined as anyone who has not yet reached their 18th birthday.
        'Children' therefore means 'children and young people' throughout
        this document.

Working Together to Safeguard Children 2010 states:

*The fact that a child has reached 16 years of age, is living independently
or is in further education, is a member of the armed forces, is in hospital,
in prison or in a Young Offenders' Institution, does not change his or
her status or entitlement to services or protection under the Children
Act 1989.*

Working Together, 1.19

1.25   The term **safeguarding** covers vetting and safer recruitment, safer
        working practices, responding to concerns, working with partner
        agencies, dealing with allegations against those responsible for children
        and other matters that may be relevant. The term **child protection** is
        used for responding to concerns where it appears that a child may have
        been harmed.

1.26   Effective child protection is essential as part of wider work to safeguard
        and promote the welfare of children. However, all agencies and
        individuals should aim proactively to safeguard and promote the
        welfare of children so that the need for action to protect children
        from harm is reduced.

1.27   The term church officer is used for anyone appointed by or on behalf
        of the Church to a post or role, whether they are ordained or lay, paid
        or unpaid.

---

[4] Adapted from the Nolan principles in The Nolan Commission Report 2001 as presented by Eileen
Shearer at the National Organiszation for the Treatment of Abusers (NOTA) conference 2006.

Each local authority is required to provide social care services for children. Locally there are a wide variety of terms, and each parish should identify the relevant department and contact details locally. This policy uses the terminology from *Working Together to Safeguard Children 2010* – **children's social care**.

Children in need

1.28 A child is a **child in need** if:

- he or she is unlikely to achieve or maintain, or have the opportunity of achieving or maintaining, a reasonable standard of health or development without the provision for him or her of services by a local authority;

- his or her health or development is likely to be significantly impaired, or further impaired, without the provision for him or her of such services;

- he or she is disabled.[5]

1.29 The critical factors to be taken into account in deciding whether a child is in need under the Children Act 1989 are:

- what will happen to a child's health or development without services being provided;

- the likely effect of services on the child's standard of health and development.

Harm and significant harm

1.30 Harm means ill-treatment or the impairment of health or development, including, for example, impairment suffered from seeing or hearing the ill-treatment of another.

1.31 The Children Act 1989 introduced the concept of **significant harm** as the threshold that justifies compulsory intervention in family life in the best interests of children, and gives local authorities a duty to make enquiries to decide whether they should take action to safeguard or promote the welfare of a child who is suffering, or likely to suffer, significant harm. It is the threshold used by the courts in deciding whether compulsory intervention into family life might be in the best interests of the child. Significant harm has no precise definition. It can be caused by a single traumatic event or a cluster of smaller incidents over time. Any concern about significant harm requires careful investigation and assessment.

1.32 There are a range of orders that a local authority may apply for and some of these grant them a share in the parental responsibility for the child. The most far-reaching of these are a Care Order, which commits the child to the care of the local authority, or a Supervision Order, which puts the child under the supervision of a local authority or probation service.

---

[5] Children Act 1989 Section 17 (10).

1.33 The court may also make private law orders if there are disputes between parents about the care of a child, or where the child needs to live with extended family or friends under the protection of the family court, but does not require the additional protection of a care order.

2 Safeguarding Policy of the Church of England

2.1 The Law and guidance cited is that for England and Wales and is up to date as at August 2110. The Church of England, in all aspects of its life, is committed to and will champion the safeguarding of children, both in society as a whole and in its own community. It fully accepts, endorses and will implement the principle first enshrined in the Children Act 1989: the welfare of the child should be paramount. The Church of England will foster and encourage best practice within its community by setting standards for working with children and young people and by supporting parents in the care of their children. It will work with statutory bodies, voluntary agencies and other faith communities to promote the safety and well-being of children. It is committed to acting promptly whenever a concern is raised about a child or about the behaviour of an adult or someone under the age of eighteen in a position of trust, and will work with the appropriate statutory bodies when an investigation into child abuse is necessary. It is also committed to the support of those who have been abused and to listening to the voices of survivors, who can help the Church learn lessons from the past.

Discussion of the principles

2.2 The statement of principles is common for children and for vulnerable adults. However, this section and the rest of this document consider only the implications for children.

2.3 We are committed to:

- the care, nurture of, and respectful pastoral ministry with, all children and adults;

- the safeguarding and protection of all children and adults;

- the establishment of safe, caring communities which provide a loving environment where there is a culture of informed vigilance regarding the dangers of abuse.

2.4 The safeguarding and protection of children is everyone's responsibility, not just parents or those who have formal responsibilities for children. Procedures and formal processes alone, though essential, will not protect children. The community, including all its members, needs to be aware of the dangers and be prepared to report concerns and take action if necessary.

2.5 The child's welfare is the paramount consideration in matters of private or public law affecting children which come before the family courts. The Church accepts and extends this principle to all areas of its work with children. Where conflicts of interest arise between the welfare of children and that of adults, it is the welfare of children that will be given priority.

2.6 **We will carefully select and train all those with any responsibility for children within the Church in line with safer recruitment principles, including the use of criminal records disclosures and registration with the relevant vetting and barring schemes.**

2.7 Vetting procedures and safer recruitment guidance for the Church of England are set out in detail in companion guidance document *Safeguarding Guidance for Safer Recruitment*. The relevant vetting and barring scheme for the Church of England is that provided by the Independent Safeguarding Authority (ISA) (See 5.7 for further details). The suitability of an applicant or nominated volunteer for work with children should not be solely dependent upon vetting checks and CRB disclosures. Someone whose CRB disclosure is clear may still be unsuitable and the other safer recruitment processes must always also be used.

2.8 In England, registration with the ISA is a statutory requirement for a number of people who work with children. Advice about how this new requirement will be phased in will be made available to each diocese via the bishop or the diocesan safeguarding adviser. (See 5.7 for further detail about the current arrangements.)

2.9 It is the policy of the Church that:

- all those who regularly work with children, including those who work on a rota, should have enhanced CRB checks and ISA registration;

- those who work only occasionally will be asked to apply for CRB checks and ISA registration if they fulfil the ISA threshold requirements;

- those who manage or supervise people who work with vulnerable groups will also be required to be ISA registered and obtain CRB checks.

2.10 **We will respond without delay to every complaint made which suggests that an adult or child may have been harmed, co-operating with the police and local authority in any investigation.**

2.11 The Church accepts that, through its workers, it is responsible for children who are entrusted to churches by their parents: in the church building, on church property and other premises being used, and during church activities. Responsibility extends to travel between places, when it is organized by the church. However, a church is not responsible for private arrangements made by parents.

2.12 The term 'complaint' can cover an allegation, disclosure or statement; something seen or something heard. The complaint need not be made in writing but, once received, it must be recorded and acted upon.

2.13 **We will seek to offer informed pastoral care with anyone who has suffered abuse, developing, with him or her, an appropriate ministry.**

2.14 The Church does not investigate allegations of abuse or neglect of children itself but refers them to the appropriate statutory agencies. The Church may need to make preliminary enquiries to establish the accuracy of information being passed to the statutory body.

2.15   If a child comes to notice as having suffered abuse in the past, church officers will notify the appropriate authorities to ensure that the matter is on record.

2.16   Support will be offered to adult survivors of child abuse, who will also be encouraged to make a statement to the police if they have not done so before. The Church has issued separate guidance on work with survivors[6].

2.17   **We will seek to challenge any abuse of power, especially by anyone in a position of trust.**

2.18   We are aware that those in positions of trust and responsibility, in the Church as elsewhere, may be subject to temptation to abuse their power and exploit or harm others. We seek to take action to deal with any abuse.

2.19   Allegations of abuse or misconduct in relation to children by church officers will be referred to the Local Authority Designated Officer (LADO) and investigated in accordance with his or her advice.

2.20   **We will seek to offer pastoral care and support, including supervision and referral to proper authorities, of any member of our church community known to have offended against a child or vulnerable adult.**

2.21   If a member of a church community comes to notice as having a conviction, caution, reprimand or warning for offences against children, or has been barred from working with children, or is considered to present a risk to children, we will seek to draw up a written agreement, where it is safe to do so. The agreement will contain safeguards as explained in detail later on. Breach of this agreement, or other concerns, may lead to a referral to the statutory agencies.

2.22   **In all these principles we will follow legislation, guidance and recognized good practice.**

2.23   This will involve, in particular, openness among those with a legitimate need to know, confidentiality for those not directly involved, and the sharing of information with the statutory authorities.

---

[6] *Responding Well to Those Who Have Experienced Sexual Abuse*, House of Bishops, 2011.

3 Definitions of forms of harm

Introduction

3.1 Children can be harmed in many ways. Where their health, physical, emotional, intellectual, spiritual or social development is damaged by other people, this is an abuse of relationships, a misuse of power and a betrayal of trust. Someone may abuse or neglect a child by inflicting harm or by failing to act to prevent harm. Children may be abused in a family or in an institutional or community setting, by those known to them, or, more rarely, by a stranger. They may be abused by an adult or adults, or by another child or children.

3.2 The fact that a child has reached the age of 16, is living independently or is in further education, is a member of the armed forces, is in hospital, in prison or a young offenders' institution, does not change his or her entitlement to protection.

3.3 Child abuse is not new, although it has been increasingly recognized, named and condemned during the course of the twentieth and into the twenty-first century. Abuse of children is much broader than sexual abuse. All abuse is a betrayal of trust and a misuse of authority and power. Church communities must be particularly vigilant to identify the inappropriate use of any religious belief or practice which may harm somebody spiritually, emotionally or physically.

3.4 Child abuse affects girls and boys, babies and young people of all ages up to 18, including children with learning difficulties, children with physical disabilities and children from all kinds of family background. It occurs in all cultures, religions and classes.

3.5 Most child abuse is perpetrated by an adult, male or female, who is well known to the child, often a family member. Such trusted adults may be in the child's community; they may be trusted professionals, leaders or members of a child's church. Abuse can be an act of commission, such as physical abuse, or omission, such as neglect or failure to protect.

3.6 Children may suffer both directly and indirectly if they live in households where there is domestic violence. Domestic violence includes any incident of threatening behaviour, violence or abuse between adults or young people, who are or who have been intimate partners, family members or extended family members, regardless of gender and sexuality. If there is domestic violence it is now accepted that there will always be at least emotional abuse of any children in the household, and there may also be direct abuse of them.

3.7 Child abuse can also be perpetrated by children against other children. This is referred to as 'peer abuse'. These child perpetrators will have greater power than their victims, perhaps due to age, gender, physique or ability. There is no clear dividing line between this form of abuse and bullying.

3.8 Child abuse can result in a child suffering significant harm[7] and the need for court proceedings to safeguard their welfare. Abuse prevents children from achieving their full potential and undermines their dignity and rights. The harm it causes will affect children while it is happening and in later life. The consequences and the pain of child abuse are almost always long-lasting and likely to affect the children when they become adults. The damage may be apparent in many aspects of their lives, including their relationships and the care of their own children. When abuse occurs within the context of the Church or by a Christian, it may affect the person's faith and spiritual development.

3.9 Recent developments in the use of computers, the internet, mobile phones and digital cameras present new challenges in educating and safeguarding children.

Statutory definitions

3.10 Child abuse has many forms. There are four identified categories of abuse described in *Working Together to Safeguard Children* 2010, from which the following definitions are taken.

3.11 Abuse and neglect are forms of maltreatment of a child. Somebody may abuse or neglect a child by inflicting harm, or by failing to act to prevent harm. Children may be abused in a family or in an institutional or community setting, by those known to them or, more rarely, by a stranger, for example via the internet. They may be abused by another adult or adults, or another child or children.

3.12 **Physical abuse** may involve hitting, shaking, throwing, poisoning, burning or scalding, drowning, suffocating or otherwise causing physical harm to a child. Physical harm may also be caused when a parent or carer fabricates the symptoms of, or deliberately induces illness in, a child.

3.13 **Sexual abuse** involves forcing or enticing a child to take part in sexual activities, not necessarily involving a high level of violence, whether or not the child is aware of what is happening. The activities may involve physical contact, including assault by penetration (for example, rape or oral sex) or non-penetrative acts such as masturbation, kissing, rubbing and touching outside of clothing. They may also include non-contact activities, such as involving children in looking at, or in the production of, sexual images, watching sexual activities, encouraging children to behave in sexually inappropriate ways, or grooming a child in preparation for abuse (including via the internet). Sexual abuse is not solely perpetrated by adult males. Women can also commit acts of sexual abuse, as can other children.

3.14 **Neglect** is the persistent failure to meet a child's basic physical and/or psychological needs, likely to result in the serious impairment of the child's health or development. Neglect may occur during pregnancy as a result of maternal substance abuse. Once a child is born, neglect may involve a parent or carer failing to:

---

[7] See section 1.5 for a discussion of significant harm.

- provide adequate food, clothing and shelter (including exclusion from home or abandonment);

- protect a child from physical and emotional harm or danger;

- ensure adequate supervision (including the use of inadequate care-givers);

- ensure access to appropriate medical care or treatment.

It may also include neglect of, or unresponsiveness to, a child's basic emotional needs.

3.15   **Emotional abuse** is the persistent emotional maltreatment of a child such as to cause severe and persistent adverse effects on the child's emotional development. It may involve conveying to children that they are worthless or unloved, inadequate, or valued only in so far as they meet the needs of another person. It may include not giving the child opportunities to express their views, deliberately silencing them or ridiculing what they say or how they communicate. Emotional abuse may feature age or developmentally inappropriate expectations being imposed on children. These may include interactions that are beyond the child's developmental capability, as well as overprotection and limitation of exploration and learning, or preventing the child participating in normal social interaction. It may also involve: seeing or hearing the ill-treatment of another, for example in domestic violence situations; serious bullying (including cyber-bullying); causing children frequently to feel frightened or in danger; exploitation or corruption of children. Some level of emotional abuse is involved in all types of maltreatment of a child but it may occur as the sole or main form of abuse.

Some special topics

3.16   Church members should be aware that, within these categories, a wide range of abuse can occur. The Government issues guidance documents or advice for several of these special topics. Among those which have been the subject of attention are:

Stranger abuse

3.17   The majority of abuse is carried out by people known to the child, but abuse can also be carried out by strangers.

Internet-related abuse

3.18   Adults may target chat rooms, social networking sites, messaging services, digital cameras, mobile phones and the internet generally in order to groom and abuse children. Children are particularly vulnerable to abuse by adults who pretend to be children of comparable ages in social networking sites and who try to obtain images or engineer meetings.[8] Children themselves can also misuse these facilities, sometimes inadvertently and sometimes with malicious intent.

---

[8] See Nicola David, *Staying Safe Online*, Grove Books, 2007.

3.19 The downloading, keeping or distributing of indecent images of children are all offences which are widely committed by adults, including by church members.

3.20 For detailed advice about protecting children from internet abuse, consult the Child Exploitation and On-line Protection Centre (CEOP), which also produces material suitable for children.

Bullying (abuse by other children)

3.21 There is no clear boundary between bullying and abuse, and a significant number of sex offenders are themselves minors. Young perpetrators of abuse are still children and are entitled to have their needs considered though steps may need to be taken to protect other children. Such cases should always be referred to the local authority children's social care service.

Children affected by gang activity

3.22 Such children are at risk of violent crime and are therefore considered vulnerable. Risks include access to weapons (including firearms), retaliatory violence and territorial violence with other gangs. Other risks include increased likelihood of involvement in knife crime, dangerous dogs, sexual violence and substance misuse.

Fabricated or induced illness

3.23 Parents and carers can induce or pretend to observe symptoms in a child which lead to unnecessary investigations or treatment.

Abuse of disabled children

3.24 Research has shown that disabled children are more likely than able-bodied children to be subjected to abuse. Disability covers not only physical disabilities of various kinds but also mental illness and learning disability.

Deliberate self-harm (e.g. overdoses, cutting, misuse of drugs or alcohol)

3.25 Local Safeguarding Children Boards vary in their approach to deliberate self-harm. It will always be appropriate to discuss such a case with the local authority children's social care. Help can also be obtained from child and adolescent mental health services (CAMHS), through the general practitioner (GP) and, sometimes, from direct access counselling services.

Domestic violence or abuse[9]

3.26 The terms 'violence' or 'abuse' are used interchangeably and carry the same meaning. Domestic violence is the abuse of adults within a household.

---

[9] See *Responding to Domestic Abuse: Guidelines for Those with Pastoral Responsibilities*, Archbishops' Council, 2006.

It need not involve physical assault to count as violence, and the adults concerned need not be married or of opposite sexes. If there are children in the household they are witnesses to the abuse and are considered to be emotionally abused at least, whether or not they are in the same room. They may also be directly affected by abuse.

Parents who are themselves vulnerable adults

3.27   It is not uncommon for the parents of children who are abused or neglected to be themselves vulnerable adults. Particularly common are problems of mental ill-health, domestic abuse and substance abuse (i.e. drugs and alcohol), often in combination. Where someone with such a difficulty is known to be a parent with a child living with them, a referral to the local authority children's social care service may be required.

Allegations of possession by evil spirits

3.28   See Ministry of Deliverance, section 6.21.[10]

Female genital mutilation

3.29   This is an offence and any suggestion that it is being sought or has been carried out should be referred to the local authority children's social care service or the police.

Child trafficking

3.30   Child trafficking is the bringing of children into the country, sometimes without proper immigration arrangements, for a variety of illegal purposes which can include domestic service, illegal adoption, organ harvesting benefit claims or prostitution. Such children may have little English. The police or local authority children's social care service should be contacted immediately if a church member comes across such a child.

Sexual exploitation and involvement in prostitution

3.31   Children can be exploited by being given rewards in return for sexual activities. Internet and other media technology may be used in the abuse. Violence, coercion and intimidation are common. Regardless of the challenging behaviours they may display, exploited children should be viewed as victims of child sexual abuse, not as criminals.

Forced marriage and honour-based violence

3.32   Disclosures of actual or possible forced marriage should not be treated as a family matter or be disclosed to family members. Local authority children's social care or the police should be contacted.

---

[10] There is also statutory guidance on Safeguarding Children from Abuse Linked to a Belief in Spirit Possession, May 2007, DCSF. www.dsf.gov.uk/everychildmatters/resources-and-practice/IG00220/.

Complex (organized or multiple) abuse

3.33   This is abuse which involves one or more abusers and a number of children. The abusers may be acting in concert, or in isolation, or may be using an institutional framework or position of authority to abuse children. The internet may also be used.

Spiritual abuse

3.34   Spiritual abuse is not covered by the statutory definitions but is of concern both within and outside faith communities including the Church.

3.35   Within faith communities, harm can also be caused by the inappropriate use of religious belief or practice. This can include the misuse of the authority of leadership or penitential discipline, oppressive teaching, or intrusive healing and deliverance ministries. Any of these could result in children experiencing physical, emotional or sexual harm. If such inappropriate behaviour becomes harmful, it should be referred for investigation in co-operation with the appropriate statutory agencies. Careful teaching, supervision and mentoring of those entrusted with the pastoral care of children should help to prevent harm occurring in this way. Other forms of spiritual harm include the denial to children of the right to faith or the opportunity to grow in the knowledge and love of God.

3.36   If anyone in the Church is uncertain whether or not abuse has taken place, he or she can contact the diocesan safeguarding children adviser or the local authority children's social care team.

4 Responsibilities of church organizations

Introduction

4.1 The Church of England, within its national institutions and within dioceses, has an obligation to support parishes and those working with children in exercising their primary responsibility for those entrusted to them. The Church is therefore committed to encouraging partnership with all statutory and voluntary agencies, other faith groups and ecumenical partnerships wherever possible. In particular, the Church recognizes the need to:

- keep abreast of research and policy developments in good safeguarding practice;

- listen and learn from victims of abuse, in order to provide the most effective support for them;

- regularly review and update Church policy and practice, taking account of the latest safeguarding information available;

- ensure that there are appropriate systems of accountability and supervision at all levels of the church's life, and that disciplinary and employment procedures are robust enough to manage risk;

- listen to those who have been abused, so that we can learn how to improve our support and care for survivors of abuse;

- ensure that all licensed ministers and lay workers are carefully selected and trained, and that their training equips them for their safeguarding responsibilities in work with children;

- provide training and support for workers who have responsibilities for children's work, so that they can undertake their tasks with confidence and without being unduly fearful of unfounded allegations being made against them.

4.2 Clear, robust procedures are essential to safeguarding. However, it is important to remember that above all it is people who protect, not procedures. The aim should be to create a culture of informed vigilance in the Church by:

- raising awareness of the issues involved in safeguarding children in the Church;

- addressing the needs of our children in all their cultural, spiritual, intellectual, racial and physical diversity;

- responding to the needs of children and adults who have been abused;

- supporting and training those who work with children, encouraging them to work together to follow good practice;

- caring appropriately for those in the church community who have abused children;

4.3   The Church seeks to minister to those who have been abused and also to those who have perpetrated abuse in the past. Inevitably, there will be tensions between the two commitments, highlighting the need for clear and comprehensive policy, procedure and good practice. The Church seeks to go beyond the minimal requirements of statute in safeguarding and to foster and promote best practice as part of its working witness to God's kingdom.

The House of Bishops

4.4   The House of Bishops will:

- be responsible for this policy, for the safeguarding of children in the Church of England and for future revisions;

- approve appropriate procedures to ensure consistency in best practice;

- appoint a bishop with lead responsibility for safeguarding children;

- ensure that a national safeguarding adviser is appointed with a clear line of accountability and a right to submit reports to the House of Bishops on safeguarding matters;

- establish minimum standards for safeguarding training for clergy, including requirements for continual ministerial training, refresher training and maintenance of records;

- ensure training is provided for senior clergy (bishops, archdeacons, cathedral deans, senior spiritual directors) in safeguarding, case recording, risk management and similar issues so that they are suitably equipped to handle allegations of abuse or misconduct by clergy, licensed lay people and other church workers;

- set minimum standards for those who are approved to conduct individual risk assessments and hold a national register of people approved to do so.

The diocese[11]

4.5   Each diocese should:

- adopt this House of Bishops' safeguarding children policy, together with any additional diocesan procedures and good practice guidelines which should be endorsed by the diocesan synod;

- provide a structure to manage safeguarding in the diocese;

- appoint a suitably qualified diocesan safeguarding children adviser, directly accountable to the diocesan bishop, and provide

---

[11] The term 'diocese' is used to cover various legal and authority structures within its geographical area. The diocesan bishop will be responsible for ensuring that the appropriate people n the diocese take responsibility for the various safeguarding children tasks.

appropriate financial, organizational and management support. The adviser must have full access to clergy files and other confidential material. The adviser may need to act as complainant under the Clergy Discipline Measure 2003. The duties of the adviser may also include work on behalf of vulnerable adults or other matters at the discretion of the diocese;

- ensure that the diocesan safeguarding children adviser is informed of any serious safeguarding situation, including any allegations made against a member of the clergy, or anyone else holding the bishop's licence, concerning misconduct in respect to children;

- include the monitoring of safeguarding in parishes as part of the archdeacons' responsibilities;

- provide access to the Criminal Records Bureau and Independent Safeguarding Authority for parishes, the cathedral, the bishop's office and the diocesan office for those beneficed and licensed clergy, paid workers and volunteers who need to obtain disclosures or to have their registration with the Independent Safeguarding Authority confirmed.[12] This should normally be by way of registering with the Criminal Records Bureau as a registered or umbrella body (see 5.7 for further details);

- keep a record of clergy and church officers that will enable a prompt response to *bona fide* enquiries. This record should include start and finish dates, all posts held and next post when known; where there have been safeguarding concerns, these should be clearly indicated on file;

- provide access to a risk assessment service so that the bishop or others can evaluate and manage any risk posed by individuals or activities within the Church;

- select and train those who are to hold the bishop's licence, in safeguarding matters;

- provide training and support on safeguarding matters to parishes, the cathedral, other clergy, diocesan organizations, including religious communities and those who hold the bishop's licence;

- provide a complaints procedure which can be used for those who wish to complain about the handling of safeguarding issues;

- share relevant information about individuals with other dioceses, other denominations and organizations or the national Church as appropriate.

---

[12] If an unregistered body wishes to use the diocese as their registered body for CRB checks and ISA registration care should be taken to check the credentials of the organization and the nature of their link with the Church. See section 3.8.

The parish[13]

4.6   Each parish should:

- adopt and implement a safeguarding children policy and procedures, accepting as a minimum the House of Bishops' Policy on Safeguarding Children or the Joint Safeguarding Principles (see page vii) but informed by additional diocesan procedures and recommended good practice, while being responsive to local parish requirements;

- appoint at least one co-ordinator to work with the incumbent and the parochial church council (PCC) to implement policy and procedures. The co-ordinator must ensure that any concerns about a child or the behaviour of an adult are appropriately reported both to the statutory agencies and to the diocesan safeguarding children adviser. It may be appropriate for this co-ordinator to be someone without other pastoral responsibility for children in the parish. The co-ordinator should either be a member of the PCC or have the right to attend the council and should report at least annually on the implementation of the policy within the parish;

- consider appointing a person, who may be different from the co-ordinator, to be a children's advocate. This should be someone whom children know they could talk to about any problems, if they so wish. It can be useful if the co-ordinator is not someone whom children know personally;

- display in church premises where children's activities take place, the contact details of the co-ordinator or children's advocate, along with the 'Childline' and 'Parentline Plus' telephone numbers;

- ensure that all those authorized to work with children are appropriately recruited according to safer recruitment practice, and are trained and supported;

- ensure that there is appropriate insurance cover for all activities involving children undertaken in the name of the parish;

- review the implementation of the safeguarding children policy, procedures and good practice, at least annually;

- if appropriate, in rural parishes or parishes held in plurality, consider joining together to implement the policy and procedures, while remembering that legal responsibility will continue to rest with the individual parishes;

- if working within Local Ecumenical Partnerships (LEPs), agree which denomination or organization's safeguarding children policy to follow, including where to seek advice in urgent situations. This

---

[13] The term 'parish' is used to denote the PCC and incumbent who are together responsible for ensuring that the child protection policy is implemented. Particular parishes may wish to use the benefice, group or team as the relevant body for practical reasons. This section should be deemed to include the cathedral of the diocese and other diocesan organizations, including religious communitites.

decision should be ratified both by the bishop and other appropriate church leaders in the partnership;[14]

- In the event of a specific safeguarding concern, ensure that all the LEP partners are notified.

Church schools

4.7   Church schools are not covered by the provisions of this policy.

- There are statutory provisions which apply to all schools, whatever sector they belong to.

- The safeguarding responsibilities of controlled and aided church schools come under the relevant local authority and Local Safeguarding Children Board.

- The safeguarding responsibilities of academies and independent schools with a church foundation come under the Local Safeguarding Children Board.

- Employees, governors and volunteers appointed by a church school should be recruited through the procedures of the relevant local authority or other suitable body, which should also process their CRB checks and ISA registration.

- Volunteers who go into a church school from their parish should normally be recruited and checked via the CRB and ISA recruitment arrangements in the diocese.[15] The school will need to confirm with the parish that these have been completed.

- Even when there is a strong link between a church school and a parish, where particular individuals hold roles in both care should be taken to distinguish and fulfil the different legal responsibilities of schools and parishes and to share information where appropriate.

- Where there is any confusion about whose responsibility it is to undertake a safeguarding action arising from a situation in the school, it is the school's responsibility to clarify this with the local authority and the diocese.

---

[14] Seperate guidance for managing safeguarding is available in Local Ecumenical Partnerships and Ecumenical Projects – in the form of a checklist – from County Ecumenical Officers and is on the Churches Together in England website.
[15] See more information at 5.7-8.

5 Promoting safer practice

Introduction

5.1   There are some key features of effective arrangements to safeguard and promote the welfare of children. These arrangements will help agencies to create and maintain an organizational culture that reflects the importance of safeguarding and promoting the welfare of children. At an organizational or strategic level, these key features[16] are:

- senior management commitment to the importance of safeguarding and promoting children's welfare;

- a clear policy stating the organization's responsibilities towards children available for all staff and volunteers;

- a clear line of accountability within the organization for work on safeguarding and promoting the welfare of children;

- clear roles for staff and volunteers;

- service development that takes account of the need to safeguard and promote welfare and that is informed, where appropriate, by the views of children and families;

- safer recruitment procedures in place;

- clear arrangements for supervision;

- clear lines of accountability;

- training for staff and volunteers on safeguarding and promoting the welfare of children for all staff working with or in contact with children and families;

- effective working with statutory and voluntary sector partners to safeguard and promote the welfare of children;

- publicly advertised arrangements for children to be able to speak to an independent person privately;

- effective information sharing.

5.2   Safer recruitment guidance is not dealt with here as it is covered in the companion volume, *Safeguarding Guidance for Recruitment*.[17] The aim of safer practice is to create a safe place for children in their involvement with a church. Church members should bear in mind that sometimes church, like school, can be a safer place for a child than their own home.

---

[16] These are based on *Safe from Harm* Home Office, 1993, and the *Statutory guidance on making arrangements to safeguard and promote the welfare of children under section 11 of the Children Act 2004* Department for Education and Skills, 2007, section 11, Guidance'.

[17] See also *Recruiting Safely*, Children's Workforce Development Council, November 2009.

5.3   The statutory basis for work with children is the following:

A person who does not have parental responsibility for a particular child but who has care of the child may (subject to the provisions of this Act [Children Act 1989]) do what is reasonable in all the circumstances of the case for the purpose of safeguarding or promoting the child's welfare.[18]

Code of Safer Working Practice

5.4   Every diocese should prepare, and every parish working with children should adopt, a code of safer working practice for church workers with children which covers the issues most likely to arise. This should have regard to the government guidance document *Guidance for Safer Working Practice for Adults who Work with Children and Young People* (Department for Children, Schools and Families for Allegations Management Advisers, 2007). This guidance provides clear advice on appropriate and safe behaviours for all adults working with children in paid or unpaid capacities, in all settings and in all contexts. It aims to:

- support safer recruitment practice;[19]

- keep children safe by clarifying which behaviours constitute safe practice and which should be avoided;

- assist adults working with children to do so safely and responsibly, and to monitor their own standards and practice;

- support managers and employers[20] in setting clear expectations of behaviour and codes of practice;

- encourage the provision of supervision and training;

- reduce the incidence of positions of trust being abused or misused;

- support employers in giving a clear message that unlawful or unsafe behaviour is unacceptable and that, where appropriate, disciplinary or legal action will be taken;

- minimize the risk of misplaced or malicious allegations made against adults who work with children.

5.5   Most church organizations will not need the full range of detail provided and should prepare a code of safer working practice which covers the majority of situations they are likely to encounter. A model code of safer working practice is given in Appendix 4.

Safer recruitment policy on vetting

5.6   This policy applies to all those who are working with children. It includes, but is not restricted to, those involved in teaching, training or

---

[18] Children Act 1989, section 3(5).

[19] This is contained in a separate document *Safeguarding Guidance for Safer Recruitment*, House of Bishops (forthcoming 2010) and in *Recruiting Safely*, Children's Workforce Development Council November, 2009.

[20] The employer will usually be the Parochial Church Council. It should be noted that the employer has the same duties to both paid staff and volunteers in respect of children for whom it is responsible.

instruction, care or supervision, and transport. See section 5.34 for mixed-age activities. It also includes those who work regularly but infrequently, for example for a few days every summer. It is the policy of the Church that all those who regularly work with children, including those who work on a rota, should have enhanced CRB checks and ISA registration. Those who work only occasionally, or who manage or supervise those who work with children, will be asked to apply for CRB checks and ISA registration if they fulfil the ISA threshold requirements.

5.7 At the time of printing, the Government has suspended full implementation of the new system for Independent Safeguarding Authority (ISA) registration, pending further review. The present arrangements for CRB initial and renewal checks and for referring matters of concern to ISA (see 7.35) continue unchanged. See Church of England safeguarding website page for up-to-date information.

5.8 Please refer to the companion document, *Safeguarding guidance for Safer Recruitment* (House of Bishops, forthcoming in 2010), for other aspects of vetting and barring policy and safer recruitment good practice. The Children's Workforce Development Council document, *Recruiting Safely* (November 2009), also gives an outline of safer recruitment.

Registration with OFSTED (the Office for Standards in Education, Children's Services and Skills)

5.9 Some parishes provide and manage groups for children under the age of six who attend regularly for more than two hours at a time or for more than fourteen days in any period of twelve months. These will need registration with OFSTED unless an exemption applies. (If the parish only lets out a building to such a provider see 5.36.) Many children's groups provided by parishes will be exempt from OFSTED registration, but will still be required to inform OFSTED of the activity. For further details consult OFSTED (through their website or information line at 08456 40404) or the children's information service of the relevant local authority.[21]

Staff–child ratios

5.10 OFSTED prescribes minimum staff–child ratios for those groups which are required to register with it. For those groups not subject to registration these ratios are advisory and should be seen as minimum standards.

0–2 years	1 person for every 3 children
2–3 years	1 person for every 4 children
3–8 years	1 person for every 8 children
over 8 years	1 person for the first 8 children and then 1 extra person for every extra 12 children

---

[21] The legal basis is *Statutory Framwork for the Early Years Foundation Stage*, Department for Education and Skills, 2007.

5.11   Each group should have a minimum of two adults and it is recommended that a gender balance be maintained if possible.

5.12   If a person who has been assigned to help staff a group is prevented from attending at short notice, there is no automatic obligation to cancel the group. It may be possible to secure the services of another suitable person or to make other appropriate temporary arrangements so that the group can still run as scheduled.

5.13   If it is proposed that a student in an appropriate discipline be included on a rota, the diocesan safeguarding children adviser should be consulted.

Staff, volunteers and helpers

5.14   Paid staff appointed to work with children should be recruited according to the principles of safer recruitment set out in the companion volume, *Safeguarding Guidance for Safer Recruitment* (forthcoming, 2010). Church organizations should consult the diocesan children's adviser, youth adviser or safeguarding children adviser before embarking on the recruitment process.

5.15   Volunteers should also be recruited according to safer recruitment principles, although it will not be necessary to consult the diocesan advisers before recruitment. Only volunteers who have been formally appointed to an appropriate role may take responsibility for children.

5.16   Other adults may help with children's groups on an occasional basis but must be accountable to an appointed worker. If they are to join the team on a regular basis they must be properly recruited as above. They will all also be asked to complete a confidential declaration.

5.17   Young people aged 16 or 17 may help with groups but must be supervised by an adult worker and cannot be counted as part of the staffing. They will also need CRB checks and ISA registration[22] if they fulfil the ISA threshold requirements. Young people aged under 16 may act as helpers but should not have responsibility for children and must be supervised. If they are on work experience a reference should be obtained from their school, with a specific question as to whether there have been any safeguarding issues. See also the next section.

Youth work

5.18   The guidance in this section is a response to the statutory duties and codes of practice now in place for youth workers in the statutory sector. These do not technically apply to the voluntary sector. However, the Church is committed, in its own guidance and codes of practice, to reflecting the good practice required in the statutory sector.

5.19   All work with those under 16 must be adequately supervised according to at least the minimum OFSTED standards as noted above. Those aged 16 and 17 do not require the same level of supervision, but should still have

---

[22] CRB checks are available in theory from age 10, the age of criminal responsibility, and ISA registration from age 16. See section 5.7 for current information on CRB and ISA registration.

an adult in charge. Although the age of 18 marks the legal division between adulthood and childhood, it may be appropriate to require a minimum three-year difference between the age of the young adult youth worker and the ages of the children he or she supervises.

5.20   Youth workers should be trained.[23] Activities and outside trips should be carefully planned, and detailed guidance sought. See section 5.31 for risk assessments.

Positions of trust

5.21   All those who work with children or who have significant contact with them and their families on behalf of the Church are in positions of trust. Staff handbooks, codes of safer working practice and contracts should make clear the importance of accepting the expectations of such work and the possible grounds for disciplinary action if they are not met:

- they will be seen as role models by the children with whom they are in contact at all times, including when they are off duty;

- all church workers should, therefore, conduct themselves in accordance with the reasonable expectations of someone who represents the Church;

- they should take care to observe appropriate boundaries between their work and their personal life. For example, they should ensure that all communications they may have with or about children are appropriate in their tone;

- they should seek advice immediately if they come across a child who may have been harmed (including self-harm) or a colleague whose conduct appears inappropriate;

- they should not expose themselves or others to material which is sexually explicit, profane, obscene, harassing, fraudulent, racially offensive, politically inflammatory, defamatory, or in violation of any British, European or international law.

5.22   It is contrary to the policy of the Church of England for those in a position of trust, including priests and youth workers among others, to have sexual or inappropriate personal relationships with those aged 16 or 17 for whom they are responsible. A breach of this is likely to be considered as a disciplinary offence. It will be referred to the local authority designated officer (LADO) and in some cases it may also constitute a criminal offence. Anyone found guilty of a criminal or disciplinary offence of this kind is likely to be dismissed and referred to the Independent Safeguarding Authority for possible barring.

---

[23] An appropriate curriculum is offered in *Equipping: Core Competencies, Learning Outcomes, Evidence of Assessment for those Working with Young People on Behalf of the Church of England*, Archbishops' Council, 2006. This includes training in safeguarding.

Cell groups or home groups

5.23 These are groups of people who meet in private houses but who have a connection with the church through the cell group. Cell groups or home groups for young people or for mixed-age groups need a degree of adult supervision if these groups are to be recognized by the church. The leaders must observe good practice and the diocesan code of safer working practice. Mixed-age cell or home groups should include members named and recruited as responsible for safeguarding young people in the group. The diocesan safeguarding children adviser should be asked to check and confirm the arrangements.

Affiliated youth groups

5.24 Sometimes a church or group of churches may set up a youth group as an independent organization. The diocesan safeguarding children adviser should be consulted and should check where the legal responsibility for such a group lies. Unless it has been set up as an independent charity it will usually be with the parent PCC. Dioceses should not make arrangements to process CRB checks or ISA registration except for groups which have a clear and demonstrable connection with the church and where they are either involved with, or satisfied by, the arrangements made for risk assessments in the event of 'positive' or 'blemished' CRB disclosure certificates.

Charity Commission

5.25 Some parishes and other church bodies will be registered charities. Guidance from the Charity Commission emphasizes the duty of care that charities have towards those who use their services and the importance of adopting and implementing appropriate policies on safeguarding. The PCC will be responsible for compliance with the Charity Commission's requirements but the diocese may be asked for technical advice on legal or practice issues.

5.26 This includes a duty to report serious cases where reputational or financial risk may occur to the Charity Commission. Guidance on this is on the Charity Commission website.[24] However, it is important to ensure that reporting to the Charity Commission does not prejudice any criminal investigation, which should always be undertaken first. In such circumstances advice should be sought from the registrar and the diocesan safeguarding children adviser. It will usually be appropriate to anonymize the report to the Charity Commission, initially. The Charity Commission may then request further details.

Transport

5.27 Transport, travel or escort arrangements to or from church activities are the responsibility of parents if they make informal arrangements among

---

[22] *Reporting Serious Incidents: Guidance for Trustees*, Charity Commission, May 2009.

themselves. They are the responsibility of the PCC if the PCC formally organizes them. It should be clearly understood by all concerned at which point responsibility for the child is passed from parent to church officer and at which point it is returned to the parent.

5.28   Diocesan safeguarding children handbooks should set clear policies for transporting children on behalf of the church. Drivers need to have appropriate insurance and to comply with the law in relation to seat belts, child seats and booster cushions. Children should travel in the back seats of cars. Appropriate arrangements, for example regarding insurance and driving qualifications, should be made by those driving minibuses on behalf of the church. Transporting children on behalf of a church is a regulated activity and CRB checks and ISA registration are required (see 5.7 for further information).

Registration and consent forms

5.29   Registration and consent forms are not required for attendance at worship, although if young children regularly attend without their parents, contact should normally be made with a parent. Contact details and special requirements should be noted for all who regularly attend other church activities, such as Sunday schools, youth groups and mixed-age activities such as choirs, and registers taken. Consent should be obtained for all activities and should include, as appropriate, consent for making and using appropriate images of children.

Health and safety

5.30   Health and safety should be managed as part of all activities. A First Aid box should be obtained and maintained on site. An accident book should be maintained at all places where children's activities take place. Buildings should be checked for health and safety regularly, at least once a year, and the results noted and reported in writing to the PCC or other appropriate church organization.

Risk assessments

5.31   Risk assessments of new and existing activities should be made, in order to identify hazards and take action to minimize risk. The same approach should be taken if buildings are hired or let for church activities involving children.

5.32   Risk assessments should be made covering outside activities including travel arrangements. If specialized activities are to be undertaken, appropriate instructors should be engaged and their credentials confirmed. However, even when specialized instructors are involved, the parish or other church body retains the duty to supervise the children

5.33   Risk assessments for individual workers are covered by the document, *Safeguarding Guidance for Recruitment*.

Mixed-age activities

5.34   Care should be taken to ensure that children in mixed-age activities such as choirs, bell ringing and serving are appropriately supervised. It is not possible to request CRB checks or ISA registration for adults in those groups unless they have specific responsibilities for children. In such groups, at least one person as well as the person leading the activity needs to be recruited safely, including a CRB check and ISA registration, and to be designated to supervise the welfare of children involved. It may be more convenient to have a team of such people taking responsibility on a rota.

Insurance

5.35   Groups working within church-organized activities will be insured through a number of different companies whose policies will be subject to various terms, conditions and exceptions. However, the majority of PCCs, parish groups, etc. will be insured with Ecclesiastical, who have made the following statement in respect of those policies they have issued for:

●   churches, in use for worship;

●   Youth groups, through the Diocesan Youth Group Scheme.

Under such policies Public Liability (Third Party) insurance, where in force, will operate to protect the interests of the insured where they are found to be legally liable for accidental death of or bodily injury to a third party or accidental loss of or damage to third party property, subject to the policy terms, conditions and exceptions.

The policy will provide an indemnity to the insured if they are held legally liable for an incident leading to accidental bodily injury or illness as a result of abuse.

It is not Ecclesiastical's intention to provide an indemnity to the perpetrator of an incident of abuse.

This statement clearly only applies to policies issued by the Ecclesiastical. Where parishes are insured with another company the position of that company should be clarified including confirmation of the scope of cover.

Policies of insurance require the insured to take all reasonable steps to prevent injury, loss or damage occurring. Failure to take such precautions may prejudice the insurance arrangements in force. A duty therefore exists upon the insured to research and adopt best practice[25] based upon current and ongoing guidelines.

It is also a condition of a policy of insurance that any incident or allegation is notified to the insurer immediately. Failure to comply with this requirement may prejudice any cover provided by the policy.

Public Liability insurance indemnity limits should be kept under regular review. Guidance is available from Ecclesiastical.

---

[25] The insurance industry uses the term 'best practice' in a sense equivalent to that of 'good practice', which is the normal term in child welfare.

Hire of premises

5.36   Many churches possess buildings which they hire out to community groups and others. Some of these may undertake work with children. Note that:

- the observance of 'reasonable care' is a standard insurance condition;

- the hiring body is required to ensure that children and adults who may be vulnerable are protected at all times, by taking all reasonable steps to prevent injury, illness, loss or damage occurring, and that they carry full liability insurance for this;

- the owner of the building (normally the PCC) has a duty to adopt best practice[26] based upon current and developing guidance.

5.37   For both one-off and regular hirings it is recommended that a written hiring agreement be used. A model form is available on the Church of England website.[27]

5.38   The hiring body should abide by their own child protection or safeguarding policy if they have one, otherwise by that of the church with whom they have a hiring agreement.

5.39   If the hiring body is required to register with OFSTED then the safeguarding children co-ordinator should ask to see the registration certificate and record that it has been seen.

Record-keeping and data protection

5.40   The Data Protection Act 1998 contains principles governing the use of personal data. These are reproduced below for convenience. Personal data should be:

- processed fairly and lawfully;

- obtained and used for specific purposes;

- adequate, relevant and not excessive;

- accurate;

- not kept for longer than is necessary;

- processed in line with a person's rights;

- secure;

- not transferred to non-UK countries without adequate protection.

5.41   The 'blue file' for clergy moves with the individual between dioceses. The original diocese should retain a separate record of clergy and church officers sufficient to be able to respond to *bona fide* enquiries at any time in the future. This should include start and finish dates, dates of CRB checks and ISA registration, all posts held and next post when known,

---

[26] See previous note.
[27] www.churchcare.co.uk

together with a flag on any database if a safeguarding problem occurred, linked with a paper record providing details of the concern and a record of what action was taken. Records should be kept secure and retained even after the people concerned have left the post or the area.

5.42   The parish should also maintain records relating to parish appointments, including a note of when a CRB check and ISA registration were obtained or checked. Records should be kept secure and retained after the people concerned have left the diocese. The national Church issues a series of records management guides to assist bishops, dioceses and parishes in good record-keeping.[28]

5.43   Records of child protection matters should be kept, together with a note of the outcome. These should be retained even if the information received was judged to be malicious, unsubstantiated or unfounded. See section 7.28.

5.44   Records of known offenders against children should be retained indefinitely, together with a copy of any agreement and reviews.

5.45   Nothing in data protection legislation seeks to limit appropriate disclosure in order to protect an individual who either is, or may be, at risk. What matters is that the process of information sharing is reasonable and proportionate.

5.46   Further advice if necessary is available from the data controller in the diocese, from the diocesan safeguarding children adviser and from the website of the Information Commissioner.

---

[28] *Cherish or Chuck? The Care of Episcopal Records*, December 2009; *Save or Delete? Care of Diocesan Records*, revised December 2008; *Keep or Bin? The Care of Your Parish Records*, revised April 2009; *Guidance Notes on Clergy Files*, revised March 2009.

6   Responding to concerns

Making referrals

6.1   If somebody believes that a child may be suffering, or is at risk of suffering, significant harm, that person should always refer the concerns to local authority children's social care services. In addition to social care, the police and the NSPCC have powers to intervene in these circumstances. Those making referrals should seek, in general, to discuss any concerns with the family and, where possible, seek their agreement to make referrals. However, this should only be done if and when such discussion and agreement-seeking does not increase the risk of significant harm, or compromise an investigation by the statutory authorities. It will often be better to wait for a strategy discussion, which will include on its agenda how and when parents should be informed. In urgent cases telephone the police.

6.2   A referral should also be made if domestic abuse comes to notice and it is known that there are children in the household. Care should be taken not to intervene directly with someone who is alleged to have committed domestic abuse as this may trigger further abuse. Seek advice from the diocesan safeguarding children adviser or telephone the specialist police unit which deals with child abuse.

6.3   Children's social care and others have been advised that personal information from referrers who are members of the public should only be disclosed to third parties (including subject families and other agencies) with the consent of the referrer.[29] Church volunteers referring children count as members of the public for this purpose.

6.4   Local Safeguarding Children Boards (LSCBs) publish procedures for use by anyone in their area who may find themselves dealing with possible abuse of a child. These procedures are usually available online and on open access. The area each LSCB covers is normally the same as that for each local authority.

6.5   The diocesan safeguarding children adviser should always be informed when a referral is made to children's social care. Records should be made and retained confidentially, even when a concern turned out to be unfounded.

6.6   The matter may proceed to a strategy discussion, or a case conference, and services may be offered or legal proceedings begun. Clergy and other church members may on occasion be asked to attend meetings, provide statements or give evidence in care proceedings or associated criminal proceedings. They should seek advice from the diocesan registrar (or the diocesan safeguarding children adviser if the registrar is not available) before doing so. They also need to be clear whether they are attending meetings simply to support someone or to contribute to assessment and planning. They should confine their contribution to what they know or

---

[29] *Working Together to Safeguard Children*, HM Government 2010, 5.35

reasonably believe at first hand. They should ensure, as far as they can, that their actions cannot be interpreted as support for one side or another in a legal dispute. They should not provide character references except in exceptional circumstances which should be discussed with the registrar or diocesan safeguarding children adviser.

Children in need

6.7   A child who is not at risk of abuse under one of the formal categories above may nevertheless qualify as a child in need. See section 1.28 for the definition.

6.8   A child in need may be referred to local authority children's social care, where possible with the consent of a parent. The referrer may be asked to contribute using the Common Assessment Framework (CAF), which is a standardized approach to the assessment of children's additional needs and decisions about how these should be met. Help with this should be sought from the diocesan safeguarding children adviser. In urgent cases, referral can be made to the child protection services even if it has not been possible to complete a CAF form.

6.9   The CAF aims to provide a simple process for a holistic assessment of children's needs and strengths, taking account of the roles of parents, carers and environmental factors on their development. Practitioners are then better placed to find appropriate support that can be agreed with children and their families. The CAF also tries to get all the appropriate services working together in an integrated way, focused on the needs of the child.

Confidentiality, information sharing and consent

6.10   Where a child or an adult is judged to be at risk of significant harm and in need of protection, it will normally be necessary to share all relevant information with the statutory agencies.

6.11   Government guidance on sharing information about the possible abuse of child is as follows:

- *You should explain to children, young people and families at the outset, openly and honestly, what and how information will, or could be shared and why, and seek their agreement.* **The exception to this is where to do so would put that child, young person or others at increased risk of significant harm or an adult at risk of serious harm, or if it would undermine the prevention, detection or prosecution of a serious crime ... including where seeking consent might lead to interference with any potential investigation.** *(our emphasis)*

- *You must always consider the safety and welfare of a child or young person when making decisions on whether to share information about them. Where there is concern that the child may be suffering or is at risk of suffering significant harm, the child's safety and welfare must be the overriding consideration.*

- *You should, where possible, respect the wishes of children, young people or families who do not consent to share confidential information. You may still share information, if in your judgment on the facts of the case, there is sufficient need in the public interest to override that lack of consent.*

- *You should seek advice where you are in doubt, especially where your doubt relates to a concern about possible significant harm to a child or serious harm to others.*

- *You should ensure that the information you share is accurate and up-to-date, necessary for the purpose for which you are sharing it, shared only with those people who need to see it, and shared securely.*[30]

6.12   There are situations where safeguarding children advisers or co-ordinators are bound to share information with the authorities or other organizations who 'need to know' according to statutory guidance and their professional standards. For guidance on individual cases the diocesan safeguarding children adviser should be consulted.

6.13   In relation to consent for medical treatment, as distinct from investigations into possible abuse or neglect, the general consensus is that children under the age of 12 cannot give informed consent, so consents will be needed for them from their parents. For older children, the Gillick decision and the Fraser guidelines become relevant. The Gillick decision was made by Scarman LJ in a House of Lords case[31] on the legality of a doctor prescribing contraception to a girl under 16 whose parent had not given consent for the treatment. It is:

As a matter of Law the parental right to determine whether or not their minor child below the age of sixteen will have medical treatment terminates if and when the child achieves sufficient understanding and intelligence to understand fully what is proposed.

A child who is deemed 'Gillick competent' is able to prevent their parents viewing their medical records. Medical staff will therefore not make a disclosure of medical records of a child who is deemed 'Gillick competent' unless consent is manifest.

Fraser Guidelines

6.14   It is lawful for doctors to provide contraceptive advice and treatment without parental consent providing certain criteria are met. These criteria, known as the Fraser Guidelines, were laid down by Lord Fraser in the House of Lord's case and require the professionals to be satisfied that:

- the young person will understand the professional's advice;
- the young person cannot be persuaded to inform their parents;
- the young person is likely to begin, or to continue having, sexual intercourse with or without contraceptive treatment;
- unless the young person receives contraceptive treatment, their physical or mental health, or both, are likely to suffer;

---

[30] *What to do if you're worried a child is being abused,* HM Government, 2006, Appendix 3, section 2.
[31] *Gillick v West Norfolk and Wisbech Area Health Authority* [1985] 3 All ER 402 (HL).

- the young person's best interests require them to recieve contraceptive advice or treatment with or without parental consent.

Although these criteria refer specifically to contraception, the principles are deemed to apply to other treatments, including abortion. The judgement in the House of Lords referred specifically to doctors, but it is commonly interpreted as additionally covering other health workers and youth workers who may be giving contraceptive advice and condoms to young people under 16. However, the application of the principle to youth workers has not been tested in court.

Serious case reviews

6.15 Local safeguarding children boards by law undertake a serious case review whenever a child dies or is seriously injured and abuse or neglect is known or suspected to be a factor. Serious case reviews are not inquiries into how a child died or who is culpable. That is a matter for coroners and criminal courts.

6.16 Clergy and other church officers could find themselves invited to contribute to a serious case review if they had sufficient individual knowledge of the child. They should consult the diocesan safeguarding children adviser who can advise on the process.

Confession

6.17 It is possible that relevant information may be disclosed in the particular context of confession.

6.18 It is in everyone's interest to recognize the distinction between what is heard in formal confession, however this might take place, which is made for the quieting of conscience and intended to lead to absolution, and disclosures made in pastoral situations. For this reason, it is helpful if confessions are normally heard at advertised times or by other arrangement or in some way differentiated from a general pastoral conversation or a meeting for spiritual direction. A stole might be worn and a liturgy should be used.

6.19 Canon Law constrains a priest from disclosing details of any crime or offence which is revealed in the course of formal confession; however, there is some doubt as to whether this absolute privilege is consistent with the civil law. Where a penitent's own behaviour is at issue, the priest should not only urge the person to report it to the police or the local authority children's social care, if that is appropriate, but may judge it necessary to withhold absolution. In such a case the priest may consider it necessary to alert the bishop to his or her decision in order to safeguard himself or herself and seek advice on the issues, though the penitent's details would not be shared without their permission. The priest might also judge it appropriate to encourage the penitent to speak personally to the bishop.

Spiritual direction

6.20 As with any other pastoral relationship, care should be taken to set parameters to the spiritual direction or spiritual accompanier relationship. It should therefore be made clear at the beginning of the relationship that disclosures of abuse will be reported and a reminder will be appropriate if it appears that such material may arise. Someone may speak of his or her own behaviour in harming a child, or the person may be an adult speaking of historical abuse from his or her own childhood. This latter is more difficult as the directee may be unwilling to reveal, or even know, names. The possibility that an abuser who is still alive may still be abusing children will likely be an imperative to encourage an adult survivor of abuse to approach the police. At the right time this may prove to be part of the healing process as well as serve to protect current children. Where children are at risk every encouragement should be given to take action to prevent further harm and the spiritual director should seek supervision in deciding how to proceed.[32]

Ministry of deliverance

6.21   It is sometimes suggested that a child is possessed by evil spirits and that this may account for behavioural issues in the child or be considered to justify harsh treatment by the parents or carers. Parents may seek the assistance of clergy or other church members. Parish priests and others should consult the bishop and should note that most parish insurance policies do not cover deliverance ministry.

6.22   This is an area of ministry where particular caution needs to be exercised, especially when ministering to someone who is in a disturbed state. The House of Bishops' guidelines on both healing and deliverance ministry[33] should be followed and cases referred to the diocesan advisers when necessary; the advisers' special expertise should be used in order to help as effectively as possible those who think they need this ministry.

6.23   The House of Bishops' guidelines on the deliverance ministry (1975) state:

The following factors should be borne in mind:

- *It should be done in collaboration with the resources of medicine.*

- *It should be done in the context of prayer and sacrament.*

- *It should be done with the minimum of publicity.*

- *It should be done by experienced persons authorized by the diocesan bishop.*

- *It should be followed up by continuing pastoral care.*

The House of Bishops' guidelines for good practice in the healing ministry (2000) state:

Deliverance. The House of Bishops' guidelines (1975) should be followed and diocesan advisers consulted when necessary.

A Time to Heal, 327

---

[32] The Stop It Now helpline provides a free confidential advice service to potential perpetrators and those concerned for them. Phone 0808 1000 900 or go to their website.

[33] See guidelines for good practice in both the healing ministry and the deliverance ministry in *A Time to Heal: A Contribution towards the Ministry of Healing*, Archbishops' Council 2000, and the associated handbook *A Time to Heal: The Development of Good Practice in the Healing Ministry: A Handbook*, Church House Publishing 2000.

6.24 The ministry of exorcism and deliverance should only be exercised by priests authorized by the bishop, who normally requires that permission be obtained from him for each specific exercise of such a ministry.

6.25 On occasions when exorcism and deliverance are administered, it is for the bishop to determine the nature of the rite and what form of words should be used.

6.26 If this ministry is sought in connection with a child the diocesan safeguarding children adviser must be involved and may need to ensure that a referral to the statutory authorities is made.

6.27 It is advisable for diocesan safeguarding children advisers to make themselves known to the diocesan ministry of deliverance team in advance of any specific case to ensure that any cases arising are appropriately brought to notice. See also the government guidance, *Safeguarding Children from Abuse Linked to a Belief in Spirit Possession*, Department for Education and Skills, 2007.

Children who have experienced abuse or trauma

6.28 Many children experience a range of disturbing and possibly frightening or uncomfortable experiences. They often struggle to understand why it has happened, want to ask questions, not always needing answers, and at times want something to be done about the situation they find themselves in. These young people will turn to someone they trust – not always, in the eyes of adults, the most obvious person – and initially test them out as to their ability to accept and hear. Guidance is available to help adults to support young people who have experienced trauma. In some situations, referral to statutory authorities or additional specialist support will be necessary.

Survivors of past abuse[34]

6.29 In the course of their work, many priests and those offering pastoral support in the Church will find themselves hearing disclosures from adults of abuse that happened to them when they were children.

6.30 There is no single, correct procedure for dealing with a disclosure of previous abuse by an adult. The wishes of the person disclosing abuse will be very important. For some adults, just being able to talk to a trusted person about the experiences can be a powerful healing event. The pastoral care of the person who has been abused should be a priority. The Church is to issue separate guidance on work with survivors.[35]

6.31 People who have committed sexual abuse against someone years ago could well be abusing children today. The individual survivor should be encouraged and supported to report the matter to the police if this has not already been done. A prosecution may or may not be possible.

---

[34] See also the chapter about 'Care for Adult Survivors in the Church', *Promoting a Safe Church: Policy for Safeguarding Adults in the Church of England*, House of Bishops, 2006.

[35] *Responding Well to Those Who Have Experienced Sexual Abuse* (working title), House of Bishops, forthcoming in 2011.

6.32   The survivor does also need to be made aware that if, the alleged abuser is known to be still working with children either in an employed or a voluntary capacity, a referral to the Local Authority Designated Officer (LADO) must be made. This can be either by the person hearing the complaint or disclosure or by the diocesan safeguarding children adviser – who must in any case be informed. If the alleged abuser is not working with children but caring for them, then either the person hearing the complaint or disclosure or the diocesan safeguarding children adviser should make a referral to children's social care. The timing of any such communication needs to be carefully judged in order to support the survivor on their journey of disclosure while if at all possible not creating a sense that all initiative has been removed from him or her completely. Professional support and consultation should always be obtained.

6.33   In some cases the subject of the allegation may have died or proved untraceable. If the Church was involved in any way, the diocese will still need to examine its actions at the time and consider whether they were appropriate in the light of what was known and good practice. The police should be consulted in case there are links with potential abusers still living or other matters of concern. In all disclosures of past abuse, a record should be made and filed in an appropriate place.

6.34   If a child comes to notice as having suffered abuse when younger, a referral will need to be made to the local authority children's social care service.

Whistle-blowing

6.35   To fulfil their commitment to safeguard and promote the welfare of children, all organizations that provide services for, or work with, children should have appropriate whistle-blowing procedures, and a culture that enables issues about safeguarding and promoting the welfare of children to be addressed. There should be particular awareness of the increased vulnerability of children in residential care, hospital settings or custodial establishments, but whistle-blowing applies in all contexts.

6.36   In addition to situations where there is a perceived risk, whistle-blowing may be necessary to highlight more general problems with unacceptable practice, performance or behaviour.

6.37   The Public Interest Disclosure Act 1998 gives workers legal protection against being dismissed or penalized as a result of publicly disclosing certain serious concerns. While the Act does not provide the same protection for volunteers, churches should endeavour to adopt the same practice of protecting the whistle-blower that is outlined in the legislation.

6.38   Volunteers and members of a congregation should be encouraged to acknowledge their individual responsibility to bring matters of unacceptable practice, performance or behaviour to the attention of the incumbent, churchwarden, parish safeguarding children co-ordinator, or a member of the PCC. Alternatively, the diocesan safeguarding children adviser or the bishop can be contacted.

7 Managing allegations against church officers

Introduction

7.1 This section considers the situation when it is alleged that a church officer[36] has:

- behaved in a way that has harmed, or may have harmed, a child;

- possibly committed a criminal offence against, or related to, a child;

- behaved in a way that indicates that he or she is unsuitable to work with children.

7.2 Allegations that fall short of these criteria may nevertheless amount to inappropriate conduct, in which case the employer[37] will need to consider whether to handle this by way of advice, supervision and training, to use disciplinary processes, or a combination of these.

7.3 There may be up to three strands in the consideration of an allegation:

- a police investigation of a possible criminal offence;

- enquiries and assessment by children's social care about whether a child is in need of protection or in need of services;

- consideration by an employer of disciplinary action in respect of the individual.

7.4 All allegations of this kind must be reported to the local authority designated officer (LADO) and the diocesan safeguarding children adviser. The LADO may arrange for an investigation by the statutory authorities which may be in conjunction with a disciplinary investigation by the employer. The LADO will work under the procedures of the local safeguarding children board (LSCB), which should be consulted. Reporting to the LADO does not transfer responsibility from the employer to take disciplinary action if appropriate. The LADO may convene one or more strategy meetings to plan the investigation; a suitable representative of the employer and the diocesan safeguarding children adviser should attend. All relevant information should be shared with those who have a legitimate need to know in the church and with the statutory agencies. Confidentiality should be maintained outside this group.

7.5 For the purposes of this procedure it makes no difference whether the person is paid or a volunteer. If the person holds the bishop's licence or Permission to Officiate then the bishop and the diocesan registrar should

---

[36] For definition of church officer, see 1.27.

[37] The employer will usually be the Parochial Church Council. It should be noted that the employer has the same duties to both paid staff and volunteers in respect of children for whom it is responsible.

also be involved. The Clergy Discipline Measure 2003, the Clergy Discipline Rules 2005 and the associated Code of Practice have specific provisions for such cases.

7.6   For more information on how to manage allegations, including the role of the LADO, see Appendix 5, *Working Together to Safeguard Children*, 2010.

Suspension

7.7   It may be necessary to suspend a church officer, as a precautionary measure, at the appropriate rate of pay for paid staff (usually full pay), pending further investigation and a hearing, if:

- their presence might impede a proper investigation;

- their presence might cause an unacceptable risk until the matter has been resolved. This could be related to, for example, inappropriate conduct or a prima facie case of violence against a child.

7.8   This suspension is a neutral act and in no way seeks to pre-empt the investigation and final decision-making.

7.9   If the alleged misconduct involves sexual abuse or other allegations of child abuse where there is a risk that the alleged perpetrator may destroy evidence it is essential that the police are consulted *before* the alleged perpetrator is informed about any suspension decision. The police must be given the opportunity to investigate first.

7.10   In cases where there is a prima facie case of serious misconduct or abuse the registrar and the diocesan safeguarding children adviser should always be consulted immediately. In the case of clergy the provisions of the Clergy Discipline Measure 2003 will need to be followed, and the Code of Practice issued in connection with the Measure consulted.[38] For clergy who are also employees, such as chaplains and diocesan officers, the employer's disciplinary code will also need to be applied.

7.11   The employer should consult the LADO; this can be undertaken by the diocesan safeguarding children adviser on the employer's behalf. The trade union representative should be informed, if appropriate. In such cases it is essential that the line manager suspending the church officer has the appropriate authority to suspend on behalf of the PCC or other employing body and that the procedure for serious misconduct or alleged serious misconduct for the particular staff group is followed.[39] If there is any doubt about the course of action then professional advice should be sought.

7.12   Unless the police have requested a delay, as soon as preliminary enquiries indicate that a church officer may have committed serious misconduct,

---

[38] The purpose of this code is to provide guidance to all who are concerned in formal clergy discipline procedures under the 2003 Measure. It does not have the force of law, but compliance with its provisions will be assumed to be in accordance with best practice.

[39] For employees, refer to the revised ACAS Code of Practice on Disciplinary and Grievance Procedures, 2009, and ensure compliance.

the allegation should be put to him or her and he or she should normally be suspended while the complaint or allegation is investigated. Failure to deal with the matter promptly and failure to suspend the church officer while the investigation is undertaken could make a subsequent dismissal unfair. The reason for this is that summary dismissal for serious misconduct implies that the employer considers the misconduct so serious that it would be impossible to allow the church officer to remain in employment. Doubt must be cast on this belief if it takes the employer a long time to put the allegation to a church officer, or if the employer can take the risk of the church officer remaining on the premises while the investigation is undertaken.

7.13   When suspending a church officer, the appropriately authorized manager should put the allegation to him or her. The church officer may be accompanied by a friend of his or her choice and it is advisable for the manager to be accompanied as well. The allegation should be put in a non-judgemental manner and there should be an explanation of how the matter will be progressed, that is, that the church officer will be suspended, if paid on the appropriate rate of pay (normally full pay) while an investigation is carried out; that it may be necessary to speak to the church officer further during the investigation before determining whether a disciplinary hearing is required. It should be emphasized that suspension is not disciplinary action in itself and does not imply guilt, rather it is a precautionary measure that is taken where serious allegations are raised and an appropriate investigation is undertaken. A record of the suspension interview should be kept in case it is necessary to refer to it at a subsequent hearing and the arrangements for suspension should also be confirmed to the church officer in writing.

7.14   At the time of suspension the church officer should be asked if he or she undertakes any other paid or voluntary work with children. Where there are other employers (paid or voluntary posts), they should be informed of the allegation, and the church officer should be informed that this will happen. He or she should also be asked whether he or she lives in a household with children (who may require protective measures).

Insurance advice

7.15   Where clergy are concerned and in all cases concerning church officers where there may be liability issues, the employer or the relevant diocese should inform the claims manager of the insurance company as soon as any incident arises that may lead to a claim. Advice should be sought about the insurance position and any steps needed to be taken to safeguard it. The claims manager will also need to keep in touch with developments. Any person accused of abuse where they have the benefit of insurance should also inform their insurance company.

Pastoral support

7.16   During the investigation the child and family will need support. A separate person will need to support the alleged perpetrator. People involved in support should be uninvolved with the investigation or disciplinary proceedings and may be chosen from outside the diocese to ensure neutrality. The police advise that it is important that these parties should not communicate with each other about the allegation so that evidence is not contaminated. In the case of allegations against a priest, the archdeacon will need to manage the impact of the investigation on the parish.[40]

7.17   These situations always require sensitive pastoral care together with the wider congregation and community. This will include overseeing appropriate communications of the situation to the congregation, advice upon which should be sought from the diocesan director of communications.

Media enquiries

7.18   The diocesan director of communications (or other appropriate communications officer) should be informed and should handle all contact with the media. Their advice will help to avoid compromising any future legal proceedings. Where the matters are likely to appear in a criminal court or tribunal the national safeguarding adviser should always be informed.

Criminal proceedings

7.19   An investigation may result in various actions. It may be shown that the person has no case to answer or they may be charged with an offence and the Crown Prosecution Service (CPS) asked to consider prosecution. The person may admit the truth of the allegation and accept a police caution.

7.20   In order for the CPS to sanction a prosecution they have to believe that there is a reasonable prospect of gaining a conviction and also that it is in the public interest to prosecute.

7.21   If it appears likely, or is known, that criminal proceedings will be brought, then normally disciplinary action other than suspension is stayed until the conclusion of those proceedings. However, if the allegation relates to a specific child, consideration must be given to protecting the interests of the child.

7.22   Requests to produce file material in court must be referred to the registrar to avoid inappropriate disclosure of personal information which may be protected by the Data Protection Act 1998.

7.23   Clergy and others should be aware of the danger of providing a character reference in criminal matters. They should avoid commenting on matters under investigation unless invited by the investigating team at a formal meeting or in a confidential discussion with the diocesan safeguarding children adviser or registrar. They should restrict themselves to known facts and firsthand knowledge.

---

[40] See Deirdre Offord, *Betrayals of Trust: Addressing the Impact on Congregations when Leaders Abuse their Positions*, Grove Books, 2009.

7.24   The statutory agencies undertaking the investigation should be asked to provide a report which can be used in disciplinary proceedings, for other decision-making or for future reference. The report, which should be agreed with their legal advisers, should include any statements which parties have agreed can be used for this purpose, a factual account of the investigation and an assessment of any continuing risk. It is helpful if the diocesan safeguarding children adviser can agree the terms of the report at the beginning of the investigation.

7.25   There are many reasons why a particular case may not come to court or may result in a finding of 'not guilty'. This does not necessarily mean there is no remaining concern. There may remain evidence of inappropriate or misguided behaviour which needs to be addressed. The advice of the statutory agencies should be sought about any continuing risk to children. It may still be appropriate in some circumstances and in accordance with legal advice to continue disciplinary action. If there remain unresolved matters of concern, either untested complaints of serious harm to a child or evidence of inappropriate behaviour by the adult, a professional risk assessment should be carried out to try to ascertain whether it is safe for the person to continue work which brings them into contact with children. Even if a charge cannot be sustained in the criminal court there may nevertheless be well-founded concerns which may mean that the person should not continue in work with children.[41] Depending on the outcome of the assessment it may be necessary to introduce a regime of conditions: training and supervision; to refer the person to the Independent Safeguarding Authority (see section 7.35); to re-deploy the person in another post; or to terminate employment.

Resignations and compromise agreements

7.26   The fact that a person tenders his or her resignation, or ceases to provide their services, must not prevent an allegation being followed up. It is important that every effort is made to reach a conclusion in all cases of allegations bearing on the safety or welfare of children, including any in which the person concerned refuses to co-operate with the process. Wherever possible, the person should be given a full opportunity to answer the allegation and make representations about it. The process of recording the allegation and any supporting evidence, and reaching a judgement about whether it can be regarded as substantiated on the basis of all the information available, should continue even if the allegation cannot be substantiated or the person does not co-operate. It may be difficult to reach a conclusion in those circumstances, and it may not be possible to apply any disciplinary sanctions if a person's period of notice expires before the process is complete, but it is important to reach and record a conclusion wherever possible.

---

[41] Criminal charges have to be proved 'beyond reasonable doubt', while the standard of proof in civil proceedings and disciplinary hearings is the lower one of 'on the balance of probabilities'.

7.27   By the same token, so-called 'compromise agreements' – by which a person agrees to resign, the employer agrees not to pursue disciplinary action, and both parties agree a form of words to be used in any future reference – must not be used in these cases without the benefit of legal advice and consideration of any safeguarding issues. In any event, such an agreement will not prevent a thorough police investigation where appropriate, nor can it override an employer's statutory duty to make a referral to the Independent Safeguarding Authority and the Charity Commission where circumstances require it.

Record-keeping in the context of allegations

7.28   It is important that employers keep a clear and comprehensive summary of any allegations made, details of how the allegations were followed up and resolved, and of any action taken, whether by the Church or by statutory agencies, and decisions reached.[42] These should be kept in a person's confidential personnel file[43] and a copy should be given to the individual, apart from third party information for which permission for disclosure has not been given. Such information should be retained on file indefinitely. The purpose of the record is to enable accurate information to be given in response to *bona fide* enquiries or any future request for a reference. It will provide clarification in cases where a future CRB Disclosure reveals information from the police that an allegation was made but did not result in a prosecution or a conviction. It will also prevent unnecessary re-investigation if, as sometimes happens, allegations resurface after a period of time.

7.29   For an allegation to be described as false, it is necessary to have evidence that disproves the allegation. This means that the allegation is unfounded.

7.30   For an allegation to be described as malicious, it is necessary to have evidence that not only disproves the allegation, but also proves a deliberate intent to deceive.

7.31   An unsubstantiated allegation is not the same as a false allegation. It simply means that there is insufficient evidence to prove or disprove the allegation. The term, therefore, does not imply guilt or innocence.

7.32   It is as important to retain records where an allegation proved to be unfounded, malicious or unsubstantiated as in other cases, so that it is on record that the allegation was known and responded to.

7.33   At the conclusion of an investigation or proceedings, a summary should be prepared noting the allegation, the enquiries made, and the outcome. Carefully considered information should be given to the person concerned in writing, and, as appropriate and possible within the limits

---

[42] The LADO may provide a standard form for this, which can be signed by the subject of the investigation with a copy supplied to him, one retained on the church file and one retained by the LADO.

[43] If a file has not previously been set up, this should be done. If there is a file this material may need to be kept in a separate section of the file, but should not be in a different file.

of confidentiality and the need not to compromise possible statutory processes, to the person making the allegation and the victim or survivor.

7.34   If files are weeded when the person leaves the church or diocese, care should be taken to retain the material noted here.

Independent Safeguarding Authority (ISA)

7.35   A referral must be made to the ISA when the employer withdraws permission for an individual to engage in work with children, or would have done so had that individual not resigned, retired, been made redundant or been transferred to a position which is not work with children because the employer believes that the individual has engaged in **relevant conduct** or satisfied the **harm test** or has committed an offence that would lead to automatic inclusion on a barred list. This is a statutory duty on all employers and a failure to refer in such circumstances is a criminal offence. Even when the duty has not been triggered, for example when the allegation is unsubstantiated, employers are empowered to refer an individual.

7.36   The referral should be made to the ISA when the employer has gathered sufficient evidence as part of their investigations to support their reasons for withdrawing permission to engage in regulated activity and, in following good practice, consulted with their LADO.

7.37   **Relevant conduct** is conduct that falls into any of these categories:

- it endangers, or is likely to endanger, a child or vulnerable adult;

- it is conduct that, if repeated against a child or vulnerable adult, would endanger them or be likely to endanger them;

- it involves sexual material relating to children (including possession of such material);

- it involves sexually explicit images depicting violence against human beings (including possession of such images);

- it is inappropriate conduct of a sexual nature involving a child or vulnerable adult.

7.38   The **harm test** is satisfied if, in the view of the relevant person (e.g. the PCC), the individual:

- may harm a child or vulnerable adult;

- may cause a child or vulnerable adult to be harmed;

- puts a child or vulnerable adult at risk of harm;

- attempts to harm a child or vulnerable adult;

- incites another to harm a child or vulnerable adult.

7.39   A person will be automatically included on a barred list where he or she has been convicted of, or cautioned in relation to, serious criminal offences involving sexual misconduct or violence.[44] More information

---

[44] A full list of automatic barring offences is contained in Statutory Instruments SI 2009/37 and 2009/2610 and is available at www.opsi.gov.uk.

can be obtained from the diocesan safeguarding children adviser or the registrar. The ISA issues referral guidance for use in these situations.[45] There is legal cover for the sharing of information which this duty requires.[46]

Charity Commission

7.40   If the parish or other employer is a registered charity, when a referral is made to the ISA the Charity Commission should also be informed. Guidance about this is on the Charity Commission website.[47] It will usually be appropriate to anonymize the report to the Charity Commission initially. The Charity Commission may then request further details.

Archbishops' List

7.41   The Archbishops' List was set up by the Clergy Discipline Measure 2003. It is compiled and maintained jointly by the archbishops, and is kept at Lambeth Palace. A copy of the List is kept by the Archbishop of York at Bishopthorpe. It is not open for public inspection, but is available to the President of Tribunals and diocesan bishops and registrars. It lists only ordained clergy.

7.42   There are five categories of names in the List:

(a)   those on whom a penalty under the Measure has been imposed (or those who were liable to a censure under the Measure's predecessor, the Ecclesiastical Jurisdiction Measure 1963);

(b)   those who were deposed from Holy Orders under the Ecclesiastical Jurisdiction Measure 1963;

(c)   anyone who has executed a deed of relinquishment under the Clerical Disabilities Act 1870;

(d)   anyone who has resigned following the making of a formal complaint;

(e)   those who, in the opinion of the archbishops, have acted in a manner (not amounting to misconduct) which might affect their suitability for holding preferment (i.e. any office or position requiring the discharge of spiritual duties).

7.43   The presence of a person's name on the List does not necessarily imply that the person does or does not present a risk to children. In appropriate cases, information about the facts which led to the inclusion of a person's name on the List may be obtained by authorized diocesan officers from the authorities in Lambeth and Bishopthorpe.

---

[45] ISA Referral Guidance, www.isa-gov.org/default.aspx?page=379. There is a standard form which should be used.

[46] Safeguarding Vulnerable Groups Act 2006, section 35(2).

[47] 'Reporting Serious Incidents – guidance for trustees', May 2009.

7.44 Appropriate cases will need to be referred by the diocesan bishop. For further information see the Clergy Discipline Rules 2005 and the Code of Practice under the Measure.

Reinstatement and redeployment

7.45 Careful consideration should be given to the future employment or volunteering role of the person involved. In exceptional circumstances, where a person has not been barred (such as following disciplinary action which did not lead to barring), consideration may be given to undertaking a professional risk assessment with a view to the possibility of allowing such a person to be employed or volunteer, with suitable supervision, conditions or precautions. A risk assessment would also be necessary if someone's barring was removed and they wished to participate or volunteer in church activities with children present.

7.46 Risk assessments for such purposes should only be undertaken by those with specific qualifications and experience in such work. They will normally be provided by outside organizations which are clearly independent of the diocese, have appropriately qualified staff and can provide reports which will withstand scrutiny and legal challenge.

7.47 Because of the compulsive nature of child sexual abuse, a person convicted or cautioned for any sexual offences should not work with, or be a volunteer where he or she could come into contact with, children. If the person is on a barred list it would be an offence for him or her to seek such work, or for any employer knowingly to offer it. There may also be a Sexual Offences Prevention Order (SOPO) in force, which further restricts the person's contact with children. For example, the SOPO may prohibit membership of mixed-age groups or activities in the church. An agreement should be drawn up to define the relationship between the convicted person and the church community. The advice of the police, probation service (if there is probation involvement), and children's social care (if involved) should be sought.

7.48 For people involved in pastoral or other authorized ministry, whether ordained or not, it may not be possible to provide the level of supervision required even if a particular post does not involve specific contact with children. People with such a representational ministry are regarded as trustworthy people of integrity, both by church communities and by the general public. This perception can be used by offenders to target victims. Rehabilitation to any kind of representational ministry should be approached with extreme caution; it should follow a professional risk assessment and treatment programme, and the agreement of the local safeguarding children agencies should be sought.

8 Suspected abusers and known offenders

Introduction

8.1   The term 'offender' applies only to those who have a conviction or who have accepted a caution, reprimand or warning for a criminal offence. Note that acceptance of a caution is an admission of the offence and is, therefore, equivalent to a conviction. The caution will appear on the CRB certificate. The term 'suspected abuser' is used here to refer to those who have been the subject of allegations which have not been formally substantiated but which appear to be reasonably well founded.

8.2   Under the Rehabilitation of Offenders Act 1974 some old convictions and cautions are deemed spent after a period of time, which varies according to the offence. However, for the purpose of work with children or vulnerable adults no offence is considered spent. Some of those putting themselves forward for roles in the Church which involve or could involve working with children will have convictions or cautions on their record. A CRB check containing information of this kind is termed a positive, blemished or unclear disclosure. The term is also used if other relevant material is supplied.

8.3   It is the policy of the Church of England that all people with positive or blemished CRB checks should undergo a risk assessment from a suitably qualified person. The nature of the assessment should be proportionate to the matters disclosed. It is good practice for more than one person to be involved in the process of assessing risk. The diocesan safeguarding children adviser should always be involved and will in certain cases commission a formal risk assessment. In the case of complex or borderline cases this good practice should include referral to a diocesan multi-disciplinary risk assessment panel. This can be a group drawn from the diocesan safeguarding management group.

8.4   Old, minor and unrelated offences will not prohibit otherwise suitable people from work with children. While not being complacent about risk, the Church understands that those who have done wrong are often capable of reform.

8.5   The same approach will be taken where the matters disclosed are not convictions but other relevant information which warrants or is in the process of investigation and risk assessment.

8.6   Anyone who seeks a position in the Church whose CRB or ISA registration check discloses that they are barred from working with children will be reported to the police by the CRB, as it is an offence for such a person to seek such work or for an employer knowingly to offer it.

Convicted offenders against children

8.7 Research has indicated that a higher proportion of convicted offenders against children may be found in church congregations than in the population generally.[49] It is therefore probable that many congregations will have people who have abused children among their worshippers, some of whom will be known. Not all will have committed sexual offences; some will have been guilty of neglect, physical or emotional abuse. They may still present a risk to children. The church's duty to minister to all imposes a particular responsibility to such people. However, this must not compromise the safety of children. If a congregation is generally aware of how offenders will be treated it will be easier to deal confidentially with a specific case, should one occur.

8.8 As well as people with convictions against children there are others whose position in a congregation may need to be carefully and sensitively considered to decide whether they pose a risk to children. This would include people convicted of violent or sexual offences against adults, including: domestic violence; people involved in drug or alcohol addiction; adults with a mental disorder or special needs which might, in rare cases, result in erratic behaviour. It would also include those who do not have convictions or cautions but where there are sound reasons for considering that they might present a risk to children. In appropriate cases the approach recommended below for managing sex offenders should be adopted.

Multi-Agency Public Protection Arrangements (MAPPA)

8.9 Guidance under MAPPA states that religious communities must put in place effective arrangements that allow them to ensure they are able to protect their community while allowing a sex offender to maintain his or her right to worship in a safe way when possible. An assessment of risk must be carried out, which should be done together with the police, probation services and children's social care, and with the diocesan safeguarding children adviser. The statutory agencies will provide appropriate information and guidance in this. It is important that co-operation between the church and the agencies is assured at all stages. It may be necessary on occasions to negotiate a formal information-sharing protocol between the diocese and the relevant police area and probation area; there are national guidelines available on protocols such as this.

8.10 Prison chaplains should be aware of the guidance and ensure that there is good liaison between them and the diocesan safeguarding children adviser when a sex offender leaves prison and wishes to worship in a church. Discussions may need to be held about which church is

---

[48] For ecumenical standards in handling disclosures see *Safeguarding Standards in Recruitment*, Christian Forum for Safeguarding, revised 2008 at www.churchsafe.org.uk/christian-forum.html. This gives a way of working which is recognized by more than one church denomination and when people are employed or appointed ecumenically or when more than one body is involved with the process.

[49] Unpublished research by Donald Findlater, Lucy Faithfull Foundation.

appropriate in light of an offender's needs or in light of their circumstances or the community.

8.11   The relevant section of the MAPPA guidance is as follows:

It is essential that we assist religious communities to put in place effective arrangements, which allows them to ensure they are able to protect their community whilst allowing the offender to maintain their right to worship but in a safe way. The place of worship and religious leader should be provided with sufficient information to protect their congregation.

Where an RSO [Registered Sex Offender], who has committed offences against children, or other offenders who present a risk of harm to children and/or other identified victims wishes to continue to practise their religion, through attending services and/or being part of their faith community the offender/case manager must ensure that they have fully assessed the potential risk of harm this could present.

There should always be a discussion with the offender regarding the need to protect children/identified victims (unless this places the victim at greater risk) who may also be present, at services and/or events from harm. The offender needs to be aware that information will be disclosed to the religious organisation and that they (the offender) will be required to agree to and sign a 'contract' of behaviour. Where an offender is unwilling to give this undertaking, the OM [Offender Manager] and police should consider whether to seek a restrictive condition on a licence or in a Sexual Offences Prevention Order (SOPO) to prevent the offender being in a place of worship. The outcome of this decision must be recorded [i.e. by the Offender Manager] on the ViSOR [Violent and Sex Offender Register] and the case management record.

Any breaches of the 'contract' with the offender must be reported to the offender/case manager.[50]

8.12   Note that SOPOs can be sought to control as well as to exclude an offender's involvement in a place of worship. In appropriate cases the diocesan safeguarding children adviser should explore with the police whether a SOPO condition should be sought and how it should be drafted. In this event, the diocesan bishop should be named as the supervising officer for the place of worship.

8.13   When the offender comes to notice before release, the diocesan safeguarding children adviser should explore with the probation service whether specific licence conditions should be included.

8.14   Management arrangements are likely to continue to be needed even after statutory intervention has come to an end.

Ministering to people who are known to have sexually abused children[51]

8.15   Where a sex offender is known, befriended and helped by a group of volunteers to lead a fulfilled life without direct contact with children,

---

[50] *MAPPA Guidance*, National Offender Management Service Public Protection Unit 2009, 6.5, 70.
[51] With thanks to CCPAS, the Lucy Faithfull Foundation, the Methodist Church and others.

the chances of reoffending are diminished and the church has thus an important role contributing to the prevention of child abuse.

8.16   When it is known that a member of the congregation has sexually abused a child, the diocesan safeguarding children adviser must be consulted, so that a safe course of action can be agreed in conjunction with the relevant statutory agencies. A written agreement or contract will usually be entered into with the offender which reflects research evidence about the compulsive nature of child sexual abuse.

8.17   Where a small group is formed the membership should be chosen carefully. It should include the priest or a delegated representative, a churchwarden and a representative of the children or youth work team or the parish safeguarding children co-ordinator. The diocesan safeguarding children adviser should be consulted on the constitution of the group, and training of the group may be necessary.

8.18   If the offender's victim, or in some cases the victim's family, attends the church, it is likely to be necessary to introduce the offender to another congregation. Consideration must also be given to other people who have been abused in the past.

8.19   The offender should not accept any official role or office in the church which gives him or her status or authority; a child may deem that person to be trustworthy. Some roles, for example that of churchwarden, are statute-barred to people with convictions of this kind, including offences against the person.

8.20   A meeting should be held with the offender, explaining that the appointed small group and a few others from the congregation will *need* to know the facts in order to create a safe environment for him or her. Those needing to know are likely to include the clergy, churchwardens, the safeguarding children co-ordinator and any befriending volunteers. The children's work co-ordinator will need to be informed so that he or she does not inadvertently ask the person to volunteer. The police should be invited to the meeting, in addition to the probation service, the local authority and children's social care, if they have a role.

8.21   Consideration should be given to whether, with the offender's agreement, the congregation should be told. The advantages and disadvantages of this course of action should be carefully considered, including the offender's need for protection as a vulnerable adult.

8.22   It must be made clear that no one else apart from those identified on the agreement will be informed of the facts without the offender's knowledge. The highest levels of confidentiality should be maintained unless there is a breach of the agreement and it is necessary to inform others to protect a child.

8.23   The group should offer support and friendship as well as supervision. They should endeavour to keep channels of communication open.

8.24   Those with pastoral responsibility will need to discuss with the group appropriate ways for the offender to develop and grow as a Christian without putting him- or herself and others at risk.

8.25　It will be necessary to establish clear boundaries, both to protect children and to lessen the possibility of the adult being wrongly accused of abuse. The diocesan safeguarding children adviser should assist in drafting a written agreement (referred to as a contract in the MAPPA guidance above) which might include the following elements:

- attend designated services or meetings only

- sit apart from children

- stay away from areas of the building where children meet

- attend a house group where there are no children

- decline hospitality where there are children

- never be alone with children

- never work or be part of a mixed-age group with children

- take no official role in the church.

8.26　The offender should be asked to sign the agreement. Other parties will be members of the group noted earlier. It should be made clear that as people change role, their successors will take on becoming involved.

8.27　The agreement should be enforced, and no changes made without consultation with the diocesan safeguarding children adviser and other parties involved. It should be made clear that a breach or other relevant information could lead to a referral to the police and probation service and advice that the offender attends a different church.

8.28　The agreement should include provision for close support and pastoral care.

8.29　The agreement should be reviewed at regular intervals, at least annually, with the diocesan safeguarding children adviser. A review must take the form of a face-to-face meeting with the offender and at least two members of the group. The meeting should be recorded and the record retained.

8.30　An agreement must remain in place so long as the person is a part of the congregation, whether or not they are on licence or their name appears on the Sex Offenders Register.

8.31　If the agreement is breached, the police or the probation service should be informed. In some cases it may be possible to restrict attendance at church. If the person cannot be banned because they live in the parish, the advice of the diocesan registrar should be sought and a high level of supervision maintained. It may be necessary, following consultation with the police, to inform other relevant organizations that the person presents a risk.

8.32　If the person leaves the church for another church, then the police should be involved and a new agreement should be made. If the person leaves without informing anyone where or whether they might attend for worship, the police should be informed.

8.33　Whenever possible, the agreement should be drawn up as a two-way covenant: the church will agree to levels of support and appropriate access to worship etc. while the offender agrees to the appropriate behavioural guidelines included in the agreement.

Disclosures by perpetrators of past abuse

8.34   In some cases offences only come to light after many years. In such situations, great sensitivity will be required. It must however be remembered that there may still be a substantial risk to children; therefore, the police should be informed of the offences.

A1   Statutory framework

UN Convention on the Rights of the Child

The UK Government ratified this Convention in 1992. The relevant provisions are in Article 19:

1   State parties shall take all appropriate legislative, administrative, social and educational measures to protect the child from all forms of physical or mental violence, injury or abuse, neglect or negligent treatment, maltreatment or exploitation, including sexual abuse, while in the care of parent(s), legal guardian(s) or any other person who has care of the child.

2   Such protective measures should, as appropriate, include effective procedures for the establishment of social programmes to provide necessary support for the child and for those who have care of the child, as well as for other forms of prevention and for identification, reporting, referral, investigation, treatment and follow-up of instances of child maltreatment described heretofore, and, as appropriate, for judicial involvement.

European Convention on Human Rights

The UK Government incorporated this into UK law through the Human Rights Act 1998. The relevant provisions are Articles 3 and 8:

Article 3

No one shall be subjected to torture or to inhuman or degrading treatment or punishment.

Article 8

1   Everyone has the right to respect for his private and family life, his home and his correspondence.

2   There shall be no interference by a public authority with the exercise of this right except such as is in accordance with the law and is necessary in a democratic society in the interests of national security, public safety or the economic well-being of the country, for the prevention of disorder or crime, for the protection of health or morals, or for the protection of the rights and freedoms of others.

Note that Article 8 is a limited right, which can be limited by public bodies for the greater good of either the public or an individual, if the action taken is legal, relevant and proportionate.

Statutory expectations

UK government statutes and guidance

There are many statutes, guidance documents, regulations and other statutory instruments which have a bearing on safeguarding children. This is a rapidly changing area of work and new documents are constantly being issued. A few key documents are noted here.

Working Together to Safeguard Children, HM Government, 2010. This is the most important single guidance document. It is binding on the relevant statutory organizations and is regarded as good practice in voluntary organizations. There is specific guidance for faith organizations, which is incorporated in the present document. The Church in its national, diocesan and parish structure is a group of voluntary organizations. Most church schools, however, count as part of the statutory sector.[52] Guidance documents supplementary to Working Together have been issued covering a number of specialist topics. These are not all listed here.

The following documents are listed in order of publication:

Children Act 1989. This contains the private and public law concerning arrangements for children.

Safe from Harm, Home Office circular, 1993. Advice to the voluntary sector. Although this has been largely superseded it has not been formally withdrawn or replaced.

Data Protection Act 1998. Detailed guidance is available from the Information Commissioner.

Criminal Justice and Court Services Act 2000. Schedule 4 is a comprehensive list of offences against children. It has been amended (added to) by the Sexual Offences Act 2003.

Sexual Offences Act 2003. This consolidates the law on sexual offences, including those against children, and replaces previous legislation in the field.

Children Act 2004. This increases the duties of statutory bodies to safeguard children and set up Local Safeguarding Children Boards to oversee this process. Associated with this is the Every Child Matters programme.

Clergy Discipline Rules, Stationery Office, 2005. For the Code of Practice under the Clergy Disciplines Measure 2003 see the next section.

What to do if you're worried a child is being abused, Department for Education and Skills, 2006. Non-statutory advice on action to be taken in individual cases. It is issued in both a full and a summary version and is updated regularly.

Safeguarding Children and Safer Recruitment in Education, Department for Education and Skills, 2006. This is the equivalent document for schools to Working Together.

---

[52] See section 2.5.

Safeguarding Vulnerable Groups Act 2006. This provided the legislative framework for the Independent Safeguarding Authority (see 5.7).

Safeguarding Children from Abuse Linked to a Belief in Spirit Possession, Department for Education and Skills, 2007.

Statutory Framework for the Early Years Foundation Stage, Department for Education and Skills, 2007. This applies to those facilities which must register with OFSTED.

Statutory guidance on making arrangements to safeguard and promote the welfare of children under section 11 of the Children Act 2004, Department for Education and Skills, 2007. Although this guidance, generally referred to as Section 11 guidance, is binding only on statutory bodies, it contains material helpful to voluntary bodies.

Guidance for Safer Working Practice for Adults who Work with Children and Young People, Department for Children, Schools and Families for Allegations Management Advisers, 2007. This is non-statutory advice which does not supersede advice or codes of conduct produced by employers or national bodies.

MAPPA Guidance, Ministry of Justice, 2009. Guidance on Multi-Agency Public Protection Arrangements for managing sexual and violent offenders in the community.

Recruiting Safely: Safer Recruitment Guidance Helping to Keep Children and Young People Safe, Children's Workforce Development Council, 2009. This advice document is intended particularly for voluntary organizations and small employers. It is issued in a full and a summary version.

The Vetting and Barring Scheme Guidance, Criminal Records Bureau and Independent Safeguarding Authority, 2010. Guidance notes on the implementation of the ISA registration process and the 'barred' lists. This guidance is under review, see 5.7 of main policy.

A2 Relevant Church of England documents

The following documents are listed in order of publication:

A Time to Heal: A Contribution towards the Ministry of Healing, Archbishops' Council, 2000, and the associated handbook, A Time to Heal: The Development of Good Practice in the Healing Ministry: A Handbook, Church House Publishing, 2000.

Time for Action: Sexual Abuse, the Churches and a New Dawn for Survivors, Churches Together in Britain and Ireland, 2002.

Guidelines for the Professional Conduct of the Clergy, Church House Publishing for the Convocations of Canterbury and York, 2003.

Clergy Discipline Measure 2003 Code of Practice, Church House Publishing, 2006.

Equipping: Core Competencies, Learning Outcomes, Evidence of Assessment for those Working with Young People on behalf of the Church of England, Archbishops' Council, 2006.

Promoting a Safe Church: Policy for Safeguarding Adults in the Church of England, House of Bishops, 2006.

Responding to Domestic Abuse: Guidelines for those with Pastoral Responsibility, Archbishops' Council, 2006.

Dignity at Work: Working Together to Reduce Incidents of Bullying and Harassment, Archbishops' Council, 2008.

Church of England Record Centre Records Management Guides:
> *Cherish or Chuck? The Care of Episcopal Records*, December 2009.
> *Save or Delete? Care of Diocesan Records*, revised December 2008.
> *Keep or Bin? The Care of your Parish Records*, revised April 2009.
> *Guidance Notes on Clergy Files*, revised March 2009.

Responding Well to Those who have Experienced Sexual Abuse (working title), House of Bishops, forthcoming in 2011.

A3   Other works consulted

David, Nicola: *Staying Safe Online*, Grove Books, 2007.

Offord, Deirdre: *Betrayals of Trust: Addressing the Impact on Congregarions When Leaders Abuse Their Positions*, Grove Books, 2009.

A4 Managing safeguarding children in a diocese: a model of good practice

A4.1 An audit of safeguarding work has revealed many differences of approach to this issue. The following model is offered as one effective way of organizing and supporting such work.

A4.2 **A diocesan safeguarding children management group** chaired by an independent lay person. The group might include:

- Diocesan personnel: the bishops, archdeacons, bishop's chaplain, diocesan secretary, diocesan communications officer, the diocesan children, youth and education advisers, personnel involved with clergy selection and training.

- The diocesan safeguarding children adviser.

- Professional support: diocesan registrar, representatives from local authority children's social care, police, probation, health.

A4.3 This management group should be integrated into the diocesan structures. One way of doing this is to make it a subcommittee of the bishop's council. The group should meet formally at least once a year to review diocesan policy. Further ad hoc meetings in any permutation may be called to deal with specific incidents or decision-making. The safeguarding children professionals may, for example, meet with the adviser to discuss cases and formulate advice to the bishop following positive disclosures or an investigation. The management group should maintain an overview of the arrangements for obtaining CRB checks and ISA registration. The management group should report annually to the bishop's council or diocesan synod. Some members might form a support group for the adviser and meet on a regular basis. Consideration should be given to establishing a risk assessment panel for complex cases.

A4.4 Archdeacons should always include monitoring the implementation of parish safeguarding children policies, procedures and good practice in their visitations at regular intervals and through questions in their Articles of Enquiry.

The role of the diocesan safeguarding children adviser

A4.5 The tasks shown below will usually be undertaken by one person, but they could be divided among several. Each person's role should then be carefully defined.

1 Development of policy, procedures and good practice guidelines should include:

- keeping well informed and up to date with the development of government policy, church policy and good practice;

---

[53] See 6.1 above.

- developing and regularly reviewing the diocesan safeguarding children policy, ensuring that it is easily accessible and understandable to licensed and paid workers and to volunteers.

- ensuring each parish has adopted and implemented the diocesan policy and procedures;

- monitoring and checking parish policies and providing advice and guidance on these;

- briefing the national adviser on all cases which go to public court or tribunal or which draw media attention.

2 Provision of appropriate safeguarding children training for:

- the bishop

- clergy and the bishop's staff

- clergy newly ordained or joining the diocese

- new incumbents

- readers and lay church leaders

- volunteers

- children and youth workers

- PCC members

- organists, choir leaders, music group leaders

- Tower captains of bell towers

- parish safeguarding children co-ordinators

- any other person who has responsibility for children and young people.

Evaluation, review and monitoring of the training programme

4. Case work. The diocesan safeguarding children adviser should:

- respond to requests for advice, information and guidance for individuals in the Church who are concerned about the welfare of a child;

- provide guidance and direction where there are concerns about adults who may be a risk to children;

- support individuals when a referral to local authority children's social care or the police is necessary;

- attend strategy meetings and case conferences as requested by statutory agencies. At times this will include preparing parish personnel for such meetings and attending with them;

- support parishes during a child protection or safeguarding enquiry and afterwards. This may include ensuring support is provided for others in the parish who may be affected by such an enquiry, for example volunteers or other leaders;

- work in partnership with the statutory agencies, any of whom may make the initial approach or seek information to which they are entitled;

- provide advice to the bishop or other employer on the possibility of employment or redeployment of those with convictions or continuing unresolved concerns regarding harm to a child;

- provide a risk assessment process for those with blemished or positive CRB checks and others as may be needed;

- advise when an independent risk assessment should be sought;

- draw up and regularly review agreements with those known to be a risk to children.

The nature of this work will mean that at times telephone advice will suffice. At other times the role will require meetings with individuals, the preparation of reports, or the setting up of support networks.

5. Networking

The effectiveness of the diocesan safeguarding children adviser is dependent on building professional relationships with statutory agencies:- the local safeguarding children board (LSCB), the local authority children's social care services, the local police: in particular, the child abuse investigation unit, the public protection unit, multi-agency protection panels and the local probation service.

A4.6 The diocesan safeguarding children adviser should be part of the national and regional network of diocesan safeguarding children advisers, any relevant local ecumenical or multi-faith forum; the adviser should be resourced to attend the Annual Conference of Church of England Diocesan and Methodist District Advisers.

A4.7 Within the diocese, the diocesan safeguarding children adviser will be linked with significant diocesan personnel, for example, those responsible for children's work, youth work, clergy and lay workers selection and training and social responsibility issues.

The adviser: professional requirements

A4.8 The title Diocesan Safeguarding Children Adviser is used for the person giving professional advice to the bishop, clergy and parishes, but is also in general use by those who undertake all the above tasks.

A4.9 The advice-giving part of the role must be provided by a person professionally qualified in the practice of safeguarding children.[54] He or she should be able to demonstrate professional independence and have knowledge of the structures of the Church of England and sympathy for its mission.

---

[54] Diocesan safeguarding children advisers may be qualified in various relevant professional areas, e.g. child care social work, probation, health, education, psychology or police work, but they must have experience of directly working with safeguarding issues and have undertaken specific training in child protection. They should either hold their own professional liability indemnity insurance or this should be secured by the diocese on their behalf.

The co-ordinator: administration

A4.10 A diocesan safeguarding children co-ordinator may be appointed to manage the administration, working closely with one or more advisers who provide professional advice. Unlike those giving advice, the co-ordinator would not necessarily have to be qualified in safeguarding children. He or she must ensure that all relevant information, especially anything that may be a complaint, is passed to the adviser for action. The co-ordinator should undertake basic safeguarding children awareness training.

Training

A4.11 Responsibility for safeguarding children training may be provided separately.

A4.12 The diocesan safeguarding children adviser seeks to promote best practice in safeguarding children throughout the diocese. This will include parishes and the cathedral of the diocese, and may include other diocesan linked organizations such as the Mothers Union, local theological colleges and courses, and diocesan children's events. Support may also be offered to other groups such as governors of church schools.

Accountability

A4.13 The diocesan safeguarding children adviser is accountable to the diocesan bishop, but may relate on a day to day basis to another member of the safeguarding children management group.

Finance

A4.14 The post should normally be remunerated by salary, retainer or fees and sufficient administrative support should be provided within a designated safeguarding children budget. The budget should include recognition for professional supervision and professional development.[55] When this post is provided on a *pro bono* basis all working expenses should be reimbursed and the insurance position checked.

---

[55] Certain professional advisers will be required to attend sufficient hours of additional training in order to retain their registration, e.g. with the General Social Care Council; this should include attendance at the National Safeguarding Conference annually.

A5 Model code of safer working practice

1   Guidelines for individual workers.

2   Additional guidelines for group leaders.

3   Responding to child protection concerns:

- imminent risk
- what to do if you suspect a child is at risk or has been abused.

4   Guidelines for good practice for church-sponsored activities for children and young people:

- special needs
- consent
- registration
- recommended staffing levels
- safe environment
- e-safety
- transporting children on behalf of the church.

Terminology used in this code:

- The word 'child' refers to any child or young person under the age of 18.
- The term 'group leader' is used to refer to the person with overall responsibility for a group or activity, who is answerable to the Parochial Church Council.

1 Guidelines for individual workers

You should:

- treat all children and young people with respect and dignity;.
- ensure that your own language, tone of voice and body language is respectful;
- always aim to work within sight of another adult;
- ensure another adult is informed if a child needs to be taken to the toilet; Toilet breaks should be organized for young children;
- ensure that children and young people know who they can talk to if they need to speak to someone about a personal concern;
- respond warmly to a child who needs comforting, but make sure there are other adults around;

- if any activity requires physical contact, ensure that the child and parents are aware of this and its nature beforehand;

- administer any necessary First Aid with others around;

- obtain consent for any photographs/videos to be taken, shown or displayed;

- record any concerning incidents and give the information to your group Leader. Sign and date the record;

- always share concerns about a child or the behaviour of another worker with your group leader and/or the safeguarding co-ordinator.

You should not:

- initiate physical contact. Any necessary contact (e.g. for comfort, see above) should be initiated by the child;

- invade a child's privacy while washing or toileting;

- play rough physical or sexually provocative games;

- use any form of physical punishment;

- be sexually suggestive about or to a child even in fun;

- touch a child inappropriately or obtrusively;

- scapegoat, ridicule or reject a child, group or adult;

- permit abusive peer activities e.g. initiation ceremonies, ridiculing or bullying;

- show favouritism to any one child or group;

- allow a child or young person to involve you in excessive attention seeking that is overtly physical or sexual in nature;

- give lifts to children or young people on their own or on your own;

- smoke tobacco in the presence of children;

- drink alcohol when responsible for young people;

- share sleeping accommodation with children;

- invite a child to your home alone;

- arrange social occasions with children (other than family members) outside organized group occasions;

- allow unknown adults access to children. Visitors should always be accompanied by a known person;

- allow strangers to give children lifts.

Touch

Church-sponsored groups and activities should provide a warm, nurturing environment for children and young people, while avoiding any inappropriate behaviour or the risk of allegations being made. Child abuse is harm of a very serious nature so that it is unlikely that any type of physical contact in the course of children and youth work could be misconstrued as abuse. All volunteers must work with or within sight of another adult.

Very occasionally it may be necessary to restrain a child or young person who is harming her/himself or others. Use the least possible force and inform the parents as soon as possible. All such incidents should be recorded and the information given to the church safeguarding co-ordinator.

All physical contact should be an appropriate response to the child's needs not the needs of the adult. Colleagues must be prepared to support each other and act or speak out if they think any adult is behaving inappropriately.

2. Additional guidelines for group leaders

In addition to the above the group leader should:

- ensure any health and safety requirements are adhered to;

- undertake risk assessments with appropriate action taken and record kept;

- keep register and consent forms up to date;

- have an awareness, at all times, of what is taking place and who is present;

- create space for children to talk – either formally or informally;

- liaise with safeguarding co-ordinator over good practice for safeguarding;

- always inform the safeguarding co-ordinator of any specific safeguarding concerns that arise. The safeguarding co-ordinator will liaise with the diocesan safeguarding adviser;

- liaise with the PCC.

3. Responding to child protection concerns

Do not try to deal with any child protection concern on your own. Always tell your group leader and safeguarding co-ordinator. Agree between you *who* will take *what* action and *when*.

If you are not sure if child abuse is involved, or if you have concerns about a child and you need someone to talk things over with, then again you should contact your group leader or safeguarding co-ordinator. The Local Authority Children's Social Care Duty Officer can also be a source of advice.

Always make notes about a possible child protection incident or disclosure as accurately as possible, as soon as possible. These should cover what has happened, in what context, and anything that seemed particularly significant. Quote the child's words exactly where possible. Try if possible to note from the register the child's full name, age, date of birth, address, telephone number and GP. Remember to sign the record and add your name, role, date of incident and date of the recording.

The following are all mportant points which will help anyone faced with this difficult situation:

- ensure all notes are kept in a safe place;

- if a child asks to talk in confidence **do not** promise confidentiality – you have a duty to refer a child/young person who is at risk to the statutory agencies;

- always explain that you may have to get other people to help;

- stay calm;

- listen to the child attentively;

- maintain eye contact;

- allow the child to talk, but do not press for information or ask leading questions;

- tell the child that they are not to blame for anything that has happened;

- reassure the child that they were right to tell;

- let the child know that other people will have to be told and why;

- try to explain what will happen next in a way the child can understand;

- reassure the child that he or she will continue to receive support during the difficult time to come.

Imminent risk

- If you encounter a child in a situation where the child is in imminent danger, you should act immediately to secure the safety of the child. Seek the assistance of the police and then make a referral to Local Authority Children's Social Care.

- If a child needs emergency medical attention, this should be sought immediately and directly from the emergency services. Parents, if available, should be kept fully informed.

What to do if you suspect a child is at risk or has been abused

- Agree with your group leader who will make the referral.

- Make an immediate telephone referral to the Local Authority Children's Social Care. Make it clear from the first point of contact that you are making a child protection referral.

- Describe the event or disclosure and give information about the child and family, for example the child's name, date of birth, address, telephone number and GP if known.

- Follow up your telephone call with a completed referral form (sometimes available on the Local Authority web site) or letter. If there is no acknowledgement within 48 hours, chase it.

- Remember that the child & family should, wherever possible, be informed about and consent to the referral *unless this would put the welfare of the child or another person at further risk*. If you have serious concerns, the absence of consent should not prevent a referral. The Duty Social Worker will give you advice over this if necessary.

- Be prepared to have further discussions with the social work team or the police investigation team.

- Say if you do not want your details disclosed to the family.

- For out of hours referrals, call the Emergency Social Work Team or where urgent, the police.

- Be prepared to have further discussions with the social work team or the police investigation team.

- Say if you do not want your details disclosed to the family.

- For out of hours referrals, call the Emergency Social Work Team or where urgent, the police.

4   Guidelines for good practice for church-sponsored activities for children and young people

Special needs

Welcome children and young people with special needs to the group. Try to make the premises, toilets and access suitable for people with disabilities. Ask the parent about how best to meet the child's special needs, and do not see this as the responsibility only of the child's parent. If premises are being designed or refurbished, take the opportunity to anticipate the possible special needs of future children and adults; advice is available. Disability legislation requires organizations to take reasonable steps to meet the needs of disabled people and this includes children.

Consent

Consent needs to be from a parent or person with parental responsibility. It can be from the child or young person if he or she has sufficient age and understanding in relation to the specific issue. So, for example, while parental consent is always required for a group residential holiday, a teenager would usually be able to consent to the photos from the holiday being displayed in church. You should record who has given consent for any specific activity.

Registration

A registration form should be completed for every child or young person who attends groups or activities. The form should be updated annually and include the following:

- Name and address,

- Date of birth,

- Emergency contact details,

- Medical information,

- Any special needs including activities that the child is unable to take part in.

- Consent for emergency medical treatment,

- Consent for photographs and videos if relevant.

Separate consent should be obtained for one-off events and activities, for example swimming, and also for outings, weekends away, etc.

- All personal details and consent forms must be stored securely.

- Any group that includes children who are under six years old and that meets regularly for more than two hours in any one day or for more than fourteen days a year must register their group. Please contact your local branch of OFSTED for advice.

Recommended staffing levels

The recommended minimum staffing levels for children's groups are given below. More help may be required if children are being taken out, are undertaking physical activities or if circumstances require it.

0–2 yrs	1 person for every 3 children	1 : 3
2–3 yrs	1 person for every 4 children	1 : 4
3–8 yrs	1 person for every 8 children	1 : 8
Over 8 yrs	1 person for the first 8 children then 1 extra person for every extra 12 children	

- Each group should have at least two adults and it is recommended that there should be at least one male and one female.

- If small groups are in the same room or adjoining rooms with open access between them then it is possible to have only one adult per group, dependent on the nature of the activity.

- Young people who are being encouraged to develop their leadership skills through helping should always be overseen by an appointed worker who will be responsible for ensuring that good practice and safeguarding procedures are followed and the work they are doing is appropriate to both their age and understanding.

- Adults who assist on one or two occasions must be responsible to an appointed worker. Thereafter they should become part of the team and be properly appointed through the normal recruitment process.

Safe environment

Display both the Childline telephone number in a prominent place where children and young people can see it and the Parentline Plus number for parents.

Undertake a risk assessment for each activity and in greater detail for an unusual activity or when away from the usual location.

Insurance, First Aid kit and fire precautions should be checked and a Health and Safety Check should be completed regularly with reference to the following minimum standards:

Venue

- Meeting places should be warm, well lit and well ventilated. They should be kept clean and free of clutter.

- Electric sockets should be covered.

- Toilets and handbasins should be easily available with hygienic drying facilities.

- Appropriate space and equipment should be available for any intended activity.

- If food is regularly prepared for children on the premises, the facilities will need to be checked by the Environmental Health Officer and a Food Handling and Hygiene Certificate acquired.

- Children's packed lunches should be kept refrigerated. Drinks should always be available.

- Groups must have access to a phone in order to call for help if necessary.

- Adults should be aware of the fire procedures. Fire extinguishers should be regularly checked and smoke detectors fitted throughout the premises. A fire drill should be carried out regularly.

- Unaccompanied children and young people should be encouraged not to walk to or from your premises along dark or badly lit paths.

- A First Aid kit and accident book should be available on the premises. The contents of the First Aid kit should be stored in a waterproof container and be clearly marked. Each group should designate one worker to check the contents at prescribed intervals.

- All staff and volunteer workers should be encouraged to have some First Aid knowledge and the parish should encourage access to First Aid training. A list of first aiders in the parish should be compiled and kept available. All accidents must be recorded in the accident book.

E-safety

- Ensure all electronic communications are appropriate and professional.

- If using e-technology as a group activity, ensure that an adult worker knows and understands what is happening within the group.

- Do not make any relationship with a child (other than family members) through a social networking site.

- Maintain a log of all electronic contact with individuals or groups including messaging and texting.

Transporting children on behalf of the church

Drivers

- All those who drive children on church-organized activities should have held a full and clean driving licence for over two years.

- Drivers who are not children's workers should be recruited for the task through the normal recruitment process.

- Any driver who has an endorsement of 6 points or more on their licence should inform the group leader and the church/parish safeguarding co-ordinator/church/circuit safeguarding representative.

- Any driver who has an unspent conviction for any serious road traffic offence should not transport children for the church.

- Drivers must always be in a fit state i.e. not over-tired; not under the influence of alcohol; not taking illegal substances; not under the influence of medicine which may induce drowsiness.

Private car

- Children and young people should not be transported in a private car without the prior consent of their parents or carers. This also applies to formally arranged lifts to and from a church activity.

- All cars that carry children should be comprehensively insured for both private and business use. The insured person should make sure that their insurance covers the giving of lifts relating to church-sponsored activities.

- All cars that carry children should be in a roadworthy condition.

- All children must wear suitable seat belts and use appropriate booster seats. If there are insufficient seat belts, additional children should not be carried.

- At no time should the number of children in a car exceed the usual passenger number.

- There should be a non-driving adult escort as well as the driver. If in an emergency a driver has to transport one child on his or her own, the child must sit in the back of the car.

Minibus or coach

- Workers and helpers should sit among the group and not together.

- If noise or behaviour appears to be getting out of control, stop the vehicle until calm is restored.

- Before using a minibus, ensure you know the up-to-date regulations for its use and have had a trial drive.

5. Important Telephone Numbers

(Please write in your local numbers.)

Local Agencies

Police (all non-emergency enquiries)	
Local Police Child/Family Protection Unit	
Local Council Children's Services/Social Care	
Local Emergency Social Work Team	
Local General Hospital	
CHILDLINE	0800 1111
PARENTLINE PLUS	0808 800 222

Diocesan and Parish contacts

Name		Role	Phone
Parish priest			
Group leader			
Diocesan safeguarding children adviser			
Parish safeguarding children co-ordinator			

A6   Model agreement with offender

An Agreement between JK[56] and the churches of St Luke's benefice

18 January 2010

Continue to work out your salvation with fear and trembling,
for it is God who works in you to will and to act according to his good purpose.

(Philippians 2.12–13)

St Luke's and St Andrew's Churches agree to the following:

1   To welcome J into the fellowship of our church.

2   To encourage him to grow in his faith in Christ.

3   To help him live out his new life in Christ.

4   To assist him in his desire not to reoffend.

5   To guard against J being wrongly accused of any offence.

6   To provide a local support group of Revd AB, Mr CD, Mrs EF and Mr GH who will meet regularly with J to provide pastoral support and challenge where appropriate. This will be convened by CD and will meet monthly until the first Review, and bi-monthly or at J's request thereafter. Proper notes shall be maintained and a copy of these lodged with EF or her successor as child protection officer, and the Rector.

7   To allow J to practise the organ at either church by arrangement with the Rector and in the presence of the Rector or another person nominated by him.

To this end, the following people will know about J's past offences and will offer fellowship, support, and supervision: Revd AA (incumbent), Revd AB, Revd IJ, Mrs KL, Mrs MN and Mr CD (and their successors as churchwardens), Mr PQ and Mr RS (and their successors as Churchwardens), Mr GH, Mrs EF.

No one else will be informed about J's past offences, unless there is a perceived risk to children or any other member of the public. Appropriate levels of confidentiality will be maintained.

JK agrees to the following:

1.   To sit apart from children and young people at church services and meetings.

---

[56] All names have been replaced by arbitrarily chosen initials.

2   To stay away from areas of the church where children or young people meet.

3   To ensure that he is never alone with children or young people.

4   To accept the supervision and guidance of members of the support group (see above).

5   Not to accept any official role in the church which gives him authority over others.

6   If visiting without Mrs K, not to visit the homes of church members without invitation and giving prior notice to the Rector or Revd AB.

7   Not to volunteer for any role that would involve responsibility for children.

8   Not to initiate any unsupervised contact with children.

9   To attend a cell group regularly as directed by the Rector.

10   To inform the Rector (or if the Rector is unavailable, the parish child protection officer, or failing that, another member of the Review Group) and the diocesan safeguarding shildren adviser of any arrangement to play the organ or be involved in any musical activity at another church within the diocese.

11   To inform the diocesan safeguarding children adviser (if unavailable the parish child protection officer) of any arrangement to play the organ or be involved in any musical activity at a place of worship outside the diocese, or of another religious denomination.

12   To inform any place of worship at which an arrangement has been made to play the organ or be involved in any musical activity that J is subject to an agreement with this parish.

13   To inform the diocesan safeguarding children adviser of any jobs or volunteer work applied for at other churches.

If this agreement is broken by J he understands that this may result in further measures being taken and the Police or Probation Service being informed.

The operation of this agreement will be monitored by TU or her successor as benefice child protection officer. TU will also be responsible for convening review meetings.

Review points

This agreement will be reviewed after three months, and thereafter every six months and at other times as determined by the diocesan safeguarding children adviser, or as requested by probation or police colleagues with the consent of the diocesan safeguarding children adviser. J may request a review at any time.

Reviews will take the form of a face-to-face meeting with J and at least two members of the following group and will be recorded. A copy will be given to J and a copy placed on the confidential file and supplied to the diocesan safeguarding children adviser.

Review group

AB, TU, PQ or her successor as churchwarden, GH or his successor as churchwarden, VW (or his successor in the police public protection unit), XY (or his successor in the probation service), CD.

Reviews will also take place at the following milestones:

1   On completion of an approved sex offender treatment programme, when subject to the receipt of a satisfactory report consideration will be given to J being allowed to volunteer as an occasional organist for weddings, funerals and other occasional services.

2   When discharged from probation, when consideration will be given to J being used as a regular volunteer organist for any service, subject to the advice of the professional colleagues working with J.

3   When J's name is removed from the sex offenders register.

Signed ……………………………..……………….. (Revd AB, incumbent)

Date ……………………………..……………….

Signed ……………………………..……………….. (Mr JK)

Date ……………………………..……………….

In the presence of:

…………………………………………………………………………………..

A7   Membership of the revision group

Stephen Barber (chair): Safeguarding Children Adviser, Diocese of Oxford

Peter Baldwin: Safeguarding Children Adviser, Diocese of Birmingham

Yvonne Criddle: National Safeguarding Diversity Officer

Judith Egar: Legal Adviser, National Church

Elizabeth Hall: National Safeguarding Adviser (from July 2010)

Julian Hodgson: Safeguarding Adviser, Diocese of Derby

Pearl Luxon: National Safeguarding Adviser (until July 2010)

Yvonne Quirk: The Bishop of Ely's Safeguarding Adviser

Jill Sandham: Safeguarding Adviser, Diocese of Southwark

Jean Skinner: Safeguarding Adviser, Diocese of Newcastle

A8   Acknowledgements

The group has benefited from the contributions and comments of many people, among them Michael Angell, Simon Bass (CCPAS), Beatrice Brandon, Carolyn Buckeridge, Rachel Bussey, Anthony Collins Solicitors LLP, Janet Hind, Stephen York.